# SING
## LIKE NEVER
## BEFORE

# For more content, exercises, and tips that correspond with the book visit
# SingLikeNeverBefore.com
## and enter the passcode JOY

Copyright © 2020 by Justin Stoney
*All world rights reserved*

No part of this book may be reproduced, stored in a retrieval system, or transmitted in any form or by any means electronic, mechanical, photocopying, recording or otherwise, without the prior consent of the publisher.

Published by Mission Point Press
2554 Chandler Rd.
Traverse City, MI 49696
(231) 421-9513
www.MissionPointPress.com

ISBN: 978-1-950659-75-3
Library of Congress Control Number: 2020917526

Cover art, cover design, book design, and book layout by Mark Pate

Printed in the United States of America

# SING
## LIKE NEVER BEFORE

A Creative Look at Vocal Technique &
Pedagogy for Singers & Voice Teachers

**JUSTIN STONEY**

Illustrated by
MARK PATE

### To Manny.

The faithful feline
whose noble ears patiently took in
more voice lessons than any
other cat in history.

You are forever the king of my heart.

### To Carolyn.

God's greatest gift
of friendship, love, faith,
and adventure.

You are my song of joy.

### To Mom.

Because my feeblest
efforts make you proud, my mightiest
efforts are made possible.

You are my reason for loving.

# CONTENTS

FOREWORD ........ xi
INTRODUCTION ........ xiii

## CHAPTER 1
### BREATHING
### 1

**1. THE DIAPHRAGM** ........ 3
Sing From the Diaphragm?!

**2. CLAVICULAR BREATHING** ........ 5
Get It Off Your Chest

**3. ABDOMINAL BREATHING** ........ 7
Your Big Chance!

**4. INTERCOSTAL BREATHING** ........ 9
Serious Pedagogical Concerns

**5. APPOGGIO BREATHING** ........ 11
"Dear Celebrity Diva Goddess…"

**6. BREATH SUPPORT** ........ 13
Singing's Favorite Buzzword…
More or Less

**7. FRICATIVES & BREATH SUPPORT** ........ 15
Hissy Fitness

**8. SOLAR PLEXUS** ........ 17
The Solar Plexus Also Rises

**9. SUBGLOTTIC PRESSURE** ........ 19
You've Got… to Hold… It In…

**10. RECTUS ABDOMINIS & INTERNAL INTERCOSTALS** ........ 21
Squeeze From the Bottom

## CHAPTER 2
### THE LARYNX
### 23

**11. LARYNX** ........ 25
The Elephant in the Room

**12. LARYNX STRUCTURE** ........ 27
Looks Kinda Like A…

**13. VOCAL FOLDS** ........ 29
Blessed Are Those That Cannot Be Seen

**14. VOCAL FOLD LAYERS** ........ 31
Fluffy & the Five Facets of the Folds

**15. THYROARYTENOID** ........ 33
Two Singers Walk Into a Bar…

**16. CRICOTHYROID** ........ 35
Is There a High Note Muscle?

**17. POSTERIOR CRICOARYTENOIDS** ........ 37
The UnSUNG Heroes

**18. LATERAL CRICOARYTENOIDS & INTERARYTENOIDS** ........ 39
Come Together… Right Now…

**19. FALSE VOCAL FOLDS** ........ 41
True or False QUIZ

**20. EPIGLOTTIS** ........ 43
Don't Choke!

## CHAPTER 3
### VOCAL RESONANCE & TONE
### 45

**21. SOUND** — 47
It's Out of This World

**22. PITCH** — 49
It Never Hz to Ask

**23. TIMBRE** — 51
Head Swapping

**24. RESONANCE** — 53
The PROs' Choice

**25. VOWELS & FORMANTS** — 55
A, E, I, O, U, & Sometimes WHY?!

**26. LARYNGOPHARYNX** — 57
Sing From the Throat!

**27. OROPHARYNX** — 59
Say 'AHA!'

**28. NASOPHARYNX** — 61
Hitting the Pillow & the High Notes

**29. SOFT PALATE** — 63
It's All Greek to
Mee-Meh-Mah-Moh-Moo

**30. TWANG & NASAL RESONANCE** — 65
A Nasal "Whodunit"

## CHAPTER 4
### POSTURE & ALIGNMENT
### 67

**31. FEET** — 69
A Double Threat

**32. KNEES** — 71
Knee Jerk Reaction

**33. HIPS** — 73
Shake It Till You Make It

**34. LOWER BACK** — 75
Don't Sweat the 'Theque NIQUE

**35. UPPER BACK** — 77
Sounds From a Massage Parlor

**36. SHOULDERS** — 79
The Sloth, The Hero, & The Dragon

**37. STERNUM** — 81
Stoney's Secret Singer Serum

**38. THE STERNOCLEIDOMASTOID** — 83
A Real Head-Turner

**39. NECK** — 85
The Tension Treatment Trifecta

**40. HEAD** — 87
Atlas Tugged

## CHAPTER 5
### THE TONGUE, JAW, & MOUTH
### 89

**41. THE 'NG' TONGUE POSITION** — 91
The KiNG of All Vocal Exercises

**42. TONGUE RETRACTION** — 93
Singing's Spelunker

**43. TONGUE SQUEEZING** — 95
The Knurdle-Free Diet

**44. THE NEUTRAL JAW POSITION** — 97
UHHHHH...

**45. JAW THRUSTING** — 99
Your Bark Is Bigger Than Your Underbite

**46. JAW BULGING** — 101
Where There's Croak, There's Fire

**47. JAW/TONGUE SEPARATION** — 103
Partners in Vocal Crime

**48. JAW EMBOUCHURE** — 105
The Ultimate Wind Instrument!

**49. TONGUE EMBOUCHURE** — 107
Cat Got Your Tongue?

**50. LIP EMBOUCHURE** — 109
Lips' Service

# CHAPTER 6
## VOCAL REGISTRATION
### 111

**51. WHAT IS VOCAL REGISTRATION?** 113
Let There Be... Vocal Registers!

**52. VOCAL FRY** 115
Adding Definition to the Voice

**53. CHEST VOICE** 117
Strength Comes From Within

**54. HEAD VOICE** 119
It's ALL in Your Head

**55. MIX VOICE** 121
The Spice of Vocal Life

**56. FALSETTO** 123
A Vocal Register for All Seasons

**57. FLAGEOLET** 125
Of Mice & Mentality

**58. WHISTLE VOICE** 127
Every Vocal Register Has Its Day

**59. BELTING** 129
Buckle Up & Buckle Down

**60. VOICE TYPES** 131
Facing the Facts, FAQs, & Fachs

# CHAPTER 7
## LARYNX & VOCAL FOLD CONTROL
### 133

**61. COMPRESSION** 135
MVP—Most Valuable Pedagogy

**62. DECOMPRESSION** 137
Something to SHOUT About!

**63. BALANCED COMPRESSION** 139
Goldilocks & the Three
Glottal Resistances

**64. THE NEUTRAL LARYNX** 141
Just Be Yourself!

**65. HIGH LARYNX POSITIONS** 143
Never Say Never

**66. LOW LARYNX POSITIONS** 145
Is My Larynx Boring You?

**67. DISTORTION 1** 147
Snow White & the Seven
Dwarfs of Distortion

**68. DISTORTION 2** 149
"Heigh Ho! Heigh Ho!"

**69. DISTORTION 3** 151
"Mirror, Mirror, on The Wall..."

**70. STRAIGHT TONE & VIBRATO** 153
Opposites Attract

# CHAPTER 8
## VOCAL HEALTH & SPEECH
### 155

**71. HYDRATION** 157
Show 'Em What You're Made Of

**72. CONCERNING ENTs** 159
The Return of the Sing

**73. THE SINGER'S DIET** 161
Have Your Herbal Tea & Drink It Too

**74. SMOKING & ALCOHOL** 163
A Tale of Two Pities

**75. VOCAL FITNESS** 165
It Ain't Over Till the FIT Lady Sings

**76. DEVELOPING A PRACTICE PLAN** 167
You Must Take the... "N Train"?

**77. VOCAL REST** 169
A Rested Development

**78. TOP TEN RESOLUTIONS FOR HEALTHY SPEECH 1** 171
Don't Drop the Ball

**79. TOP TEN RESOLUTIONS FOR HEALTHY SPEECH 2** 173
Could You Coo? Could You Care?

**80. TOP TEN RESOLUTIONS FOR HEALTHY SPEECH 3** 175
Auld Things Are Passed Away

# CHAPTER 9

## VOCAL PERFORMANCE & ACTING
### 177

**81. ALL SINGERS ARE ACTORS** 179
Singing's Prayer Partner

**82. IDENTIFYING THE SCENE PARTNER** 181
"You Talkin' to ME?"

**83. PLAYING THE ACTION** 183
That's Why It's Called ACTING!

**84. PLAYING THE OPPOSITE** 185
This Chapter Is Not Worth Reading

**85. SONG MONOLOGUE WORK** 187
To Sing or Not to Sing?

**86. BREATHING THE PERFORMANCE** 189
Take My Breath Away

**87. TRYING TO MAKE A GOOD IMPRESSION** 191
That Still, Small Voice

**88. SINGING FROM THE EYES** 193
The EYES Have It

**89. NERVES & PERFORMANCE ANXIETY** 195
Stress & Skivvies

**90. LIVING IN THE MOMENT** 197
I'm Not Kindling!

# CHAPTER 10

## SINGING FROM THE SOUL
### 199

**91. TAKING THE FIRST STEP** 201
Forget the Difference

**92. AM I TOO OLD TO SING?** 203
The Old Man & the Glee

**93. SINGING IS A SPORT** 205
If Music Be the Food of Love…

**94. VOCAL FRIENDSHIP** 207
What Are Friends For?

**95. VOCAL SCARS** 209
But My Voice Will Always Heal Me

**96. PERFECTIONISM** 211
Bless This Mess

**97. SINGING IS A GIFT** 213
Lame Duck Precedent

**98. "MAKING IT" AS A SINGER** 215
If Joy Shines…

**99. THE VOCAL JOURNEY** 217
Practice Makes Perfect

**100. "MAKE A JOYFUL NOISE!"** 219
Found In the Being Found

INDEX 222
ACKNOWLEDGMENTS 225
ABOUT THE AUTHOR 226

was blind but now I see

# FOREWORD

I don't think of myself as a singer... NEVER have... or even as an actor who sings. Of course, there were a few (desperate) occasions when I'd stray far out on a limb and actually audition for a musical... but, unsurprisingly, those didn't end well. Truth is, I had learned from a very young age that singing was not—and would likely never be—my thing. In school, I was That Kid. You know the one. The kid who music teachers would single out just before an assembly/choral performance with the soul-crushing admonition, "Tony, you just mouth the words." But my humiliation in those moments always took a backseat to my confusion, because I think I thought I was pretty good. Plus, I really did love to sing! And though that love never dissipated, due to my newfound insecurity, my vocalizing went quickly and permanently underground.

So, luckily (?), over the course of my thirty-five-year career, I mostly managed to steer clear, sidestep, dodge, bob, weave, and otherwise avoid further opportunities to relive my childhood embarrassment.

Cut to:

A few years ago, when, for reasons I will never comprehend, I was offered the role of Tewfiq Zakaria in the new musical *The Band's Visit*. After picking myself up from the floor, brushing off my bewilderment, and graciously declining, I promised them that I would happily compile a list of nine or ten other actors who they would do well to consider for the part. Musical guys. Singers! Actors who sing. Singers who act. Actor-singers who act and sing—really well—at the same time. They weren't listening. I informed them that, as much as I adored the material, I. simply. could. not. do. it. At the first table read, I was given the name and number of the vocal coach they'd arranged for me to visit during the rehearsal period. Justin Stoney.

And...

It was a game changer. As is this book!

The approach is beautifully structured. And the bedrock is joy. The physiological/anatomical components are explained and demonstrated in a thoroughly accessible, demystifying way, and are then integrated into the psychological and emotional. For me, this amounts to a healthy and long overdue deprogramming. Dread dissolved into dynamism. Tension into transformation. There are many, many valuable lessons and gems to be gleaned from Mr. Stoney's technique... not the least of which is patience. With ourselves, our collaborators, our growth, our process, and our goals.

Thanks to the author—my coach—Justin Stoney, I attained a goal I'd NEVER allowed myself to imagine: A Tony Award... for Best Performance by an Actor in a Musical for *The Band's Visit*! What are the odds?!

*Tony Shalhoub*

**TONY SHALHOUB**
*Actor and Singer*
Tony Award and Emmy Award Winner

# INTRODUCTION

Anyone who has ever been courageous enough to sing knows that it is one of the most satisfyingly soulful, frustratingly fulfilling, and endlessly exhilarating pursuits known to humankind. Like any of the best things in life, singing is as rewarding as it is challenging. I know that you've experienced this, or else you would never have picked up a book called Sing Like Never Before.

When I discovered my God-given calling to teach voice, I knew I had found something worthy of my life's devotion: to help as many people as possible to be transformed by their singing. Throughout my career, I've given tens of thousands of voice lessons to countless singers and voice teachers from all across the world. And if I've learned anything from our studies together, it's that our vocal journeys are intimately connected with our inner journeys. It has become abundantly clear to me that the possibilities of the human voice keep uncanny time with the rhythms of the human soul. They can't be separated if we try.

If you're like me, then you not only love singing, but you also love learning about it. Yet, often when we pursue singing's numerous complexities, we are left feeling defeated. Much of the joy, passion, creativity, humor, fun, and life that drew us to singing in the first place starts to get lost.

I was very aware of this when I embarked on my six-year journey to write Sing Like Never Before. While I knew it would be ambitious, I also knew that a singing book ideally must not be confined to the technical. Instead, it should represent the many varied components that make up our complete and holistic singing experience. That's why I hope that in this book you will find:

**TECHNICAL** tools that improve the details and nuances of your vocal technique.

**SCIENTIFIC** principles that expand your understanding of how the voice works.

**VISUAL** illustrations that make vocal concepts come alive.

**CREATIVE** imagery, stories, and anecdotes that make singing ideas memorable to you.

**PRACTICAL** tips that highlight specific areas of focus as you practice.

**COMEDIC** scenes that bring laughter and a merry heart to your singing life.

**SOULFUL** passages that add inspiration, wisdom, and encouragement to your vocal journey.

Feel free to read this book from cover to cover if you'd like. Or, you can skip around to topics that interest you the most. I trust that you will use it as a reference tool, as a practice resource, and as a source of motivation for many years to come.

The one thing that I ask of you is this: please don't ever lose your joy and your passion for singing. If any part of this book helps you to know yourself and your voice more deeply, then you have helped me to achieve my life's mission. After all, this book was written for YOU. Written with dawn-cracking enthusiasm among the invigorating sips of Upper West Side coffeehouse mornings. Written with city-sleepless persistence amidst sideways glances at the lonely writer sitting in NYC craft beer pubs. And written (at any and all hours) under the rolled-eyed gaze of a Maine Coon cat wondering what could possibly be so important. In all of these moments... I thought of you. And what I wouldn't give to see you **"Sing Like Never Before."**

JUSTIN STONEY

# CHAPTER 1
*BREATHING*

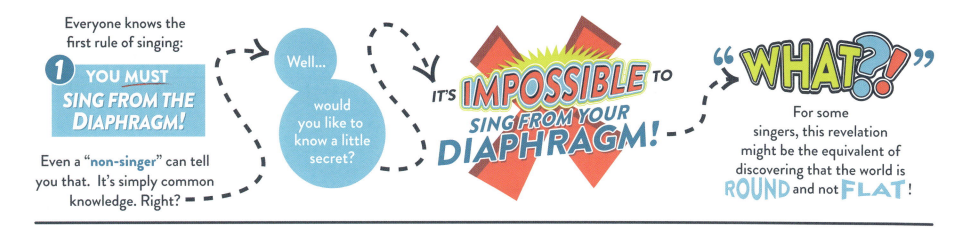

The **DIAPHRAGM** is the body's primary breathing muscle. It has a thin, sheetlike shape that divides the torso between the chest and the abdomen. The diaphragm attaches just beneath the sternum in the front of our bodies and just below the rib cage in the back.

Before we breathe in, the diaphragm has a round shape. That is, it takes on a dome-like appearance when it is relaxed. Upon inhalation, the diaphragm activates and becomes flat. This downward contraction creates a pressure system that causes air to be sucked into the lungs like a vacuum.

Understanding how the diaphragm works can really rock the boat for many singers, so let's explore it! Inhales occur when the diaphragm is muscularly active. Exhales occur when the diaphragm is relaxed and passive. Thus, the diaphragm muscle actively inhales. It doesn't actively exhale. And, of course, we don't sing on an inhale. We sing on an exhale! (If you ever do sing on an inhale, you'll make a very strange gasping sound.) So, if you've ever had trouble following the advice to sing from the diaphragm, now you know why. It's as difficult as sailing off of the Earth!

But what do people mean when they say to "sing from the diaphragm"? Well, generally they mean that our exhalations should come from a deep and low place in the torso. Also, these exhalations should be very relaxed and controlled. These are, in fact, some great pieces of advice! So, even if breathing for singing works a little differently than many people think, the guidance we've received throughout our travels may still serve us well.

No matter what direction we take, the diaphragm is most certainly a very important breathing muscle for singing. It is both a voluntary and involuntary muscle. This means that the diaphragm works involuntarily when we don't think about it. But, we can also control it in a voluntary way by thinking about it. This voluntary control allows us to decide when to inhale, when to exhale, and how much air to take in. As we'll see in the coming sections, maximizing the diaphragm's efficiency prepares our voices for their smoothest sailing!

**To sing like never before**, we must make waves by casting off some Old World vocal myths. While it may not be possible to sing from the diaphragm, it's very possible to sing like never before. And so—we set sail! On a vocal expedition that's destined to expand our horizons, our diaphragms, and our souls!

 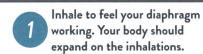 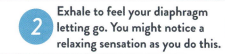 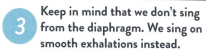

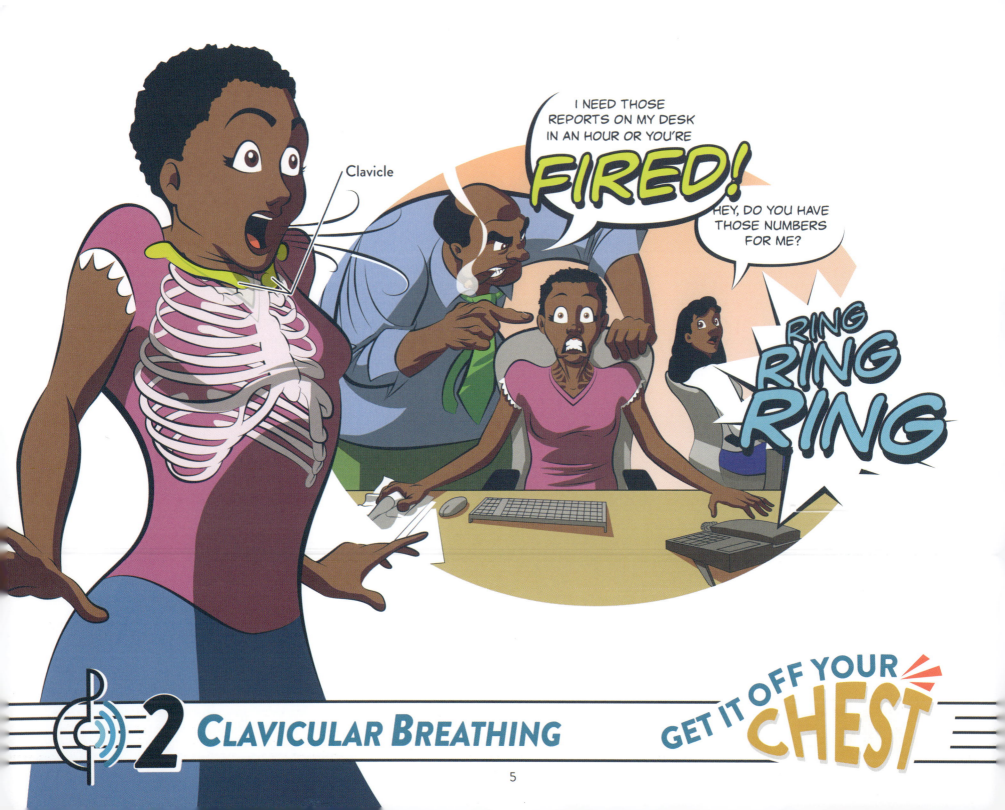

So, you've decided to kick back, relax, and read a nice soothing book about vocal technique?
Well, hopefully it doesn't stress you out too much, but this book will occasionally ask you to try new things and participate!
Don't  though. Just take a breath. In fact, start by taking the **BIGGEST** breath you can possibly take!

READY? ➔  SET? ➔  INHALE!

...so...what happened? Likely, you *lifted your chest and shoulders*. If so, you've just experienced **CLAVICULAR BREATHING!**

---

## CLAVICULAR BREATHING (chest breathing) occurs when the upper torso lifts to create space in the lungs for inhalations. This includes the chest, shoulders, and clavicle. *Clavicle* is the anatomical term for the collarbone. Clavicular breathing sometimes feels like the most natural breath for many people because it creates so much space in the upper body. However, there are several reasons why it is generally thought to be the least advantageous breathing method for singing.

### TENSION
The clavicle is very close in proximity to several neck muscles. So, clavicular breathing naturally runs the risk of causing some neck tension. Tension in the neck usually impacts the larynx. We need our larynxes to be free when we sing, or else our sounds are quite likely to be strained. That's why it's important to get off to a good start with our breathing by not involving the upper body.

### TOO MUCH AIR
Next, clavicular breathing actually gives us the most amount of air. Just like our opening example, when we take the biggest breath we can possibly take, it's definitely a clavicular breath. The problem is, good vocal technique doesn't actually require as much air as we'd imagine. In fact, filling the lungs to maximum capacity usually makes singing harder rather than easier. Ironically, singers often run out of air more quickly with full lungs simply because it is much more difficult to control the exhalation.

### STRESS
Inhaling high into the body also can induce the stress response. For example, imagine someone having a panic attack. Are they taking too much air or too little? Too much! In fact, it's rather off-base to tell a panicking person to take a deep breath. The human body's relaxation function is the result of slow, smooth exhalations. So, someone in a fit of anxiety is usually having trouble letting their breath out slowly as opposed to taking it in. Singing is also done on slow, smooth exhalations. This is one of the reasons that singing can be such a relaxing, healing, and joyful experience. How amazing that the kind of exhalation that makes us peaceful is the same kind that makes our singing work the best!

All of this said, there are some singers that do use chest breathing successfully. It's just a matter of controlling its release in a slow and relaxed way. So, if that's you, then know that you can still use chest breathing as long as you are using it efficiently and in a controlled fashion. In the coming sections, we will explore some breathing systems that tend to have more advantages than chest breathing. However, no matter which breathing system works for you, it's good to remember that any time you practice singing, you also practice your body's relaxation function!

**To sing like never before**, clavicular breathing should not add any unwanted stress. So, whenever you're feeling anxious, don't bottle it up. Get it off your chest!

---

 Make sure that your inhalations do not cause any tension or rigidity in the neck muscles.

 Remember that singing actually becomes harder when taking the biggest breath you can.

 If chest breathing is causing you tension and stress, then practice breathing lower in the body.

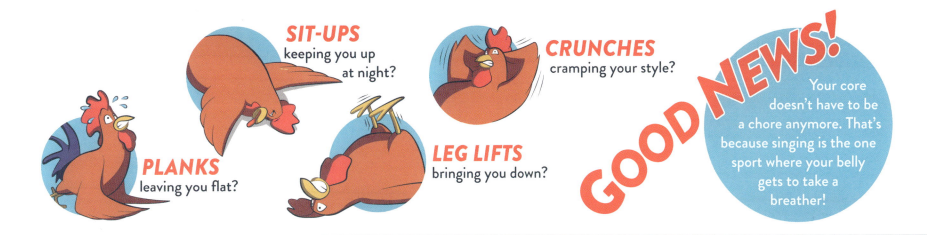

**ABDOMINAL BREATHING** (belly breathing) occurs when the abdomen releases and relaxes during inhalation. The *transverse abdominis* is the deepest muscle of the abdomen. During inhalations, it releases to allow the diaphragm to descend more deeply. During more active exhalations, it can be contracted to draw the belly inwards.

To feel this, place a hand on your abdomen. Expand your abdomen outward as you inhale. Then, let your abdomen fall inward as you exhale. Try not to effortfully take in or forcefully expel the air, but rather allow it to flow in and out. Ideally, there should be *no other movement* except for the expansion and contraction of the abdomen. If so, then you've discovered belly breathing!

Abdominal breathing is advantageous for singing because it allows inhalations to be taken with optimal efficiency by isolating the diaphragm. This ensures that we are not adding any unwanted extraneous movement to our breathing system. Since the abdominal muscles are located deep in the torso, they can be used for breathing without inviting tension into the neck, larynx, or shoulders. Abdominal breathing also brings in *less* air than clavicular breathing. Starting with less air dramatically reduces the tendency to "push" the voice (excessively increase its volume).

For some, abdominal breathing may seem unnatural at first. But, that's probably just because we're thinking about it! Whenever we're conscious of our breathing, it's very common to go to extremes. Belly breathing, though, most often occurs when we're not conscious of it. For example, it probably happens on its own while you're watching a television program, sleeping in a cozy bed, or reading a vocal book. The challenge for singing is to gain consciousness over a part of our breathing that is usually unconscious.

**To sing like never before**, let's take a few deep breaths as we review all the advantages of belly breathing. It isolates the diaphragm. It invites an ideal amount of air into the body. It allows us to breathe in a low and grounded way. So, now that you've got the lowdown on belly breathing, feel free to relax and let things hang out a bit. After all, this is your chance!

1. Observe your breathing in very relaxed settings. Is your abdominal breathing at work?

2. Practice allowing your belly to release with every inhale and gently contract with every exhale.

3. Experiment with these sensations during your vocal exercises and song work.

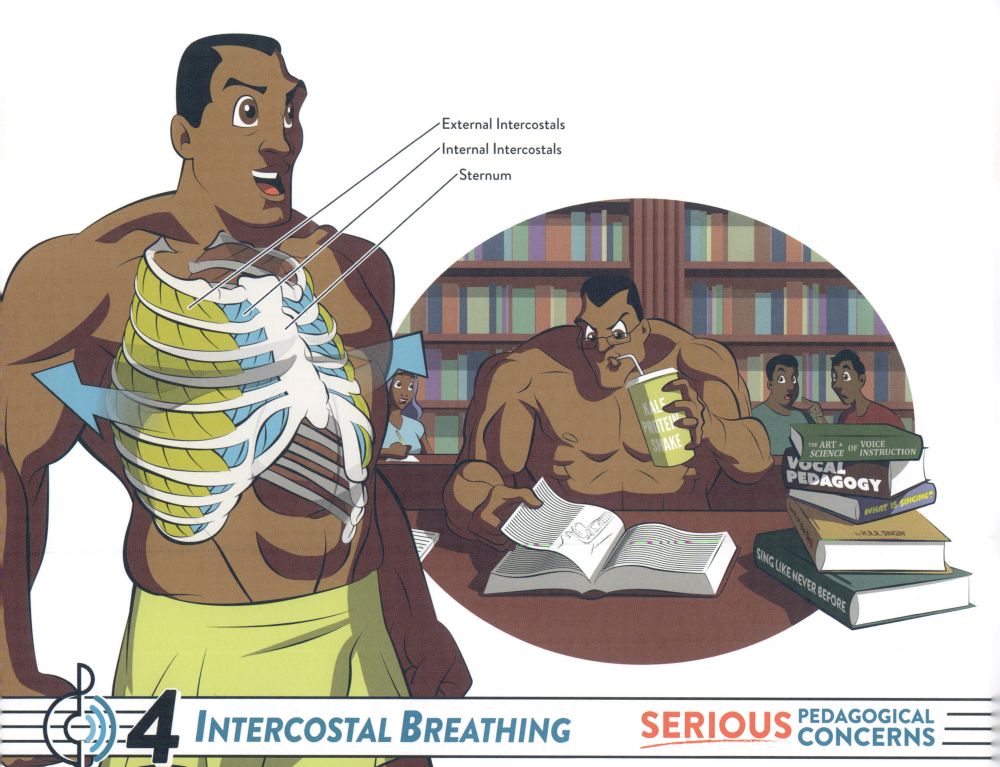

Now that we've explored the ins and outs of Belly Breathing, a few rather serious pedagogical concerns are probably perplexing the psyches of some shirtless singers:

> **WHAT IF I HAVE TO SING SHIRTLESS WITH THOUSANDS OF ADORING FANS SCREAMING MY NAME?**
> **WON'T EVERYONE STARE AT MY BELLY INSTEAD OF GAZING AT MY MEGAWATT SMILE?**
> **HOW WILL BELLY BREATHING AFFECT RECORD SALES IF NOBODY CAN APPRECIATE MY SIX PACK ABS?**

These queries will indubitably make for edifying research topics and copious academic discussions at vocal symposiums one day soon. In the meantime though—there's thankfully another way to breathe!

**INTERCOSTAL BREATHING** (rib breathing) occurs when the rib cage expands during inhalation. This movement is caused by the *external intercostals*, which run between each rib. When these muscles are engaged, they expand the distance between each rib to open the rib cage. This expansion helps air to be drawn into the lungs with or without any movement in the abdomen.

Rib breathing complements the diaphragm's work by offering the lungs more overall room to expand. While the diaphragm is active during every breath we take, belly breathing creates space below the diaphragm to assist its downward movement. On the other hand, rib breathing creates space around the perimeter of the lungs to assist their inflation.

Rib breathing is especially important for singers who face the challenge of singing and dancing simultaneously. In these situations, it is almost essential for dancers and other athletic movers to use intercostal breathing. This ensures that the core can remain engaged for movement while still allowing efficient breathing for singing.

Some other singers may simply find rib breathing to be the easiest and most natural variety of breathing based on their own unique physiology. If that's you, then go with it! Breathing technique ultimately comes down to gaining deliberate control of what to expand or contract and when to do it.

To experience rib breathing, place one hand on the side of your rib cage. Place another hand on your belly. Inhale and allow your rib cage to open and expand sideways. With a little practice, you should be able to move your ribs without moving your belly or chest. If you can isolate the movement of your rib cage, then you've discovered rib breathing!

**To sing like never before**, it's very helpful to have more than one way to breathe. Otherwise, some of us would find ourselves performing a pirouette with a protruding paunch. Rib breathing offers an alternative breathing strategy for those who rely on a firm core. Or for those who are worried about... *ahem*... pedagogy.

  Experience rib breathing by placing a hand on your ribs and expanding them as you inhale.  Place a hand on your abs and explore how rib breathing can be done *without* ab movement.  Practice rib breathing, especially if you need to dance or move athletically while singing.

> Your voice sounds amazing!
> But, would you please stop breathing the way you breathe? My voice teacher says it's bad...
> Love,
> Your Concerned Fan

We've explored **stressed chests**, **flab abs**, and **the rib cage** onstage. Yet, vocalists can actually succeed using any of these inhalation methods. Every singer is different and must choose what works best for their instrument. So, there's truly no ✅right or ❌wrong way to breathe. Nevertheless, beginning singers and celebrity singers alike yearn to know if there's a "**best**" breath? In fact, there is! It has historically been known as **APPOGGIO BREATHING**.

*APPOGGIO BREATHING* is a combination of abdominal breathing and intercostal breathing. The word "appoggio" comes from the Italian verb "appoggiare," which means "to lean." With appoggio, the lower torso (abdominals, lower rib cage, and lower back) inflates like a balloon during inhalation. Then, the upper torso (sternum, upper rib cage, and chest) leans gently atop this "balloon" during exhalation. When we exhale to sing, the goal is to avoid deflating the balloon too quickly. This requires the sternum to remain upright to ensure that breath pressure is managed beneath it.

Try it! Begin by lifting your sternum into a confident, yet relaxed posture. Then, place one hand on your abdomen and the other on your lower rib cage. Inhale into both your abdomen and rib cage at the same time. Ideally, only your rib cage, abdomen, and lower back should expand. Keep in mind that these expansions should be subtle and small—never forced. The goal is not to expand these areas to full capacity, but rather to allow them to open in an easy and natural way.

You'll immediately begin to experience how TWO breathing systems are better than one! Abdominal breathing offers a relaxed inhalation and space for your diaphragm to descend. Rib cage breathing offers your lungs an opportunity to expand without creating tension in the upper body or neck. Appoggio breathing doesn't just create an ideal inhalation, but the chance for an ideal exhalation as well. Too much belly contraction? No problem. Your rib expansion counteracts this. Too much rib cage collapse? Not to worry. Your abs can remain expansive to prevent overly forceful exhalations. This partnership between your abs and ribs allows for control, balance, and efficiency during exhalations. Your final product should be relaxed inhalation followed by a smooth exhalation—both originating from a place that feels quite low in the torso.

**To sing like never before**, appoggio breathing deserves to be the center of attention for its superior performance. Nevertheless, not every singer breathes the same way. So, while appoggio breathing might work well for you, you don't have to write to your vocal idol. Then again, maybe she'll thank you in her award speech!

  Appoggio breathing has historically been regarded as the optimal breathing technique for singing.  Place a hand on your ribs and abdomen. Allow them to expand in a relaxed way as you inhale.  Keep your sternum lifted (but not rigid) as you exhale gradually, slowly, and smoothly to sing.

 **6 Breath Support** SINGING'S FAVORITE  WORD...MORE OR LESS

If you could be a fly on the wall during a voice lesson, then you'd probably overhear some of the following advice:

YOU NEED TO WORK ON YOUR BREATH SUPPORT.

NOTHING IS MORE IMPORTANT IN SINGING THAN BREATH SUPPORT!

YOU'LL NEVER HIT THAT HIGH NOTE UNLESS YOU USE MORE BREATH SUPPORT!!!

Even a fly can figure out that **Breath Support** is singing's favorite BUZZWORD. So, what is it... more or less?

**BREATH SUPPORT** is the physical resistance of the exhalation in order to regulate air as it moves through the vocal folds. After expanding for inhalation, the body naturally returns to its resting state rather quickly upon exhalation. However, breath support asks the body to maintain much of its initial expansion as the exhalation takes place. This reduces the exhalation's forcefulness and also provides control over it for steady release.

Breath support is famous for being one of vocal technique's most important skills. Yet, it's often a victim of its own success. The term "breath support" is a vocal buzzword that is used so frequently and so haphazardly that its meaning is often obscured, confused, or misapplied.

The most common and harmful mistake is to associate *more* breath support with *more* breath, *more* breath force, and *more* breath effort. However, when breath support is executed properly, it usually creates circumstances in which *less* air, *less* force, and *less* effort are used. In short, more breath support equals less breath.

So, how do you achieve effective breath support? Start by making sure that your exhalations are controlled and not forced. This means not letting your sternum shove downward. It means not letting your rib cage collapse forcibly. It means not letting your abdominals contract inward too quickly. When these aspects of breath support are addressed, your voice will learn that it can actually do more while expending less.

Breath support's ultimate purpose is to ensure that an ideal balance of airflow and pressure is used to achieve any given vocal task. Many times, less force and effort is required than we initially think. So, as you sing your most challenging vocal tasks, ask yourself: "How much breath and effort do I *really* need for this?" Your answer will guide you towards your optimal breath support.

**To sing like never before**, we must remember that singing doesn't require massive amounts of air. Instead, it requires the small, smooth, steady airflow that happens whenever we use more breath support! So, confusing buzzwords can "shoo!" For even the fly on the wall understands that breath support means less is more...

...more or less.

**1** Find breath support by keeping your sternum, ribs, and abdomen fairly expansive as you sing.

**2** Remember that most vocal skills require much less breath force than we instinctually assume.

**3** Practice some of your vocal challenges while inviting your body to use less air than normal.

# 7 Fricatives & Breath Support

## HISSSSSSSY FITNESS

Sure, you could certainly charm some combative cobra. Or, you could prevent some presumptuous pooch from drooling on your turf.

But, perhaps the best (and safest) reason to practice your Hissing is to master your

**HISSING** is the sound made by the S consonant. S is a variety of consonant known as a fricative. *Fricatives* are consonants formed by air filtering through spaces in the mouth that have been narrowed by the lips, teeth, and tongue. The S consonant is created when air passes between the tongue tip and the *hard palate* (roof of the mouth). Other fricatives include F, SH, and TH. But, let's look at the hiss!

Place the tip of your tongue on your hard palate and exhale through the S consonant. Try to hold the hiss for about ten seconds. Notice that air cannot escape your body as quickly as usual. Instead, you've created an air pressure system that helps keep most of the air in your lungs as you exhale in a slow, smooth fashion. This is the very definition of breath support!

We've already learned that the combination of the belly and rib cage establishes ideal conditions for inhalation. Let's now explore some ways that the hiss can help us create the exhalation:

### HISSING AND ABDOMINALS

Place a hand on your belly. Begin by firmly exhaling all of your air. Then, inhale and try the hiss. You'll again notice that the hiss doesn't allow your belly to come inwards as quickly as the more aggressive breath. This simulates the experience of breath support within the abdominal breathing system.

### HISSING AND RIBS

To experience this further, place your hands on your rib cage. Try another firm exhalation. You should notice that your rib cage collapses quite quickly. Inhale again and follow it with the hiss. Notice how your rib cage doesn't descend as fast as with the firm exhalation. This simulates the experience of breath support within the intercostal breathing system.

### HISSING AND STAMINA

Finally, hissing can also be used for building breath stamina. Most professional singers can hiss for anywhere between 30 and 75 seconds. Challenge yourself to sustain your hiss for at least twenty seconds, and you'll notice immediate improvements to your stamina, control, and even vocal range. You can even try a hiss anytime during your practice of vocal exercises or songs to ensure that you have "checked in" with your optimal breath support.

**To sing like never before**, breath support is perhaps best experienced by practicing your hissing. Snakes will admire you. Dogs will respect you. But, most importantly, your voice will thank you!

1. Use the hiss or other fricative consonants (F, SH, and TH) to experience breath support.

2. As you hiss, notice that your rib cage and abdominals have less tendency to collapse.

3. Time your hissing practice to see if you can gradually increase both stamina and control.

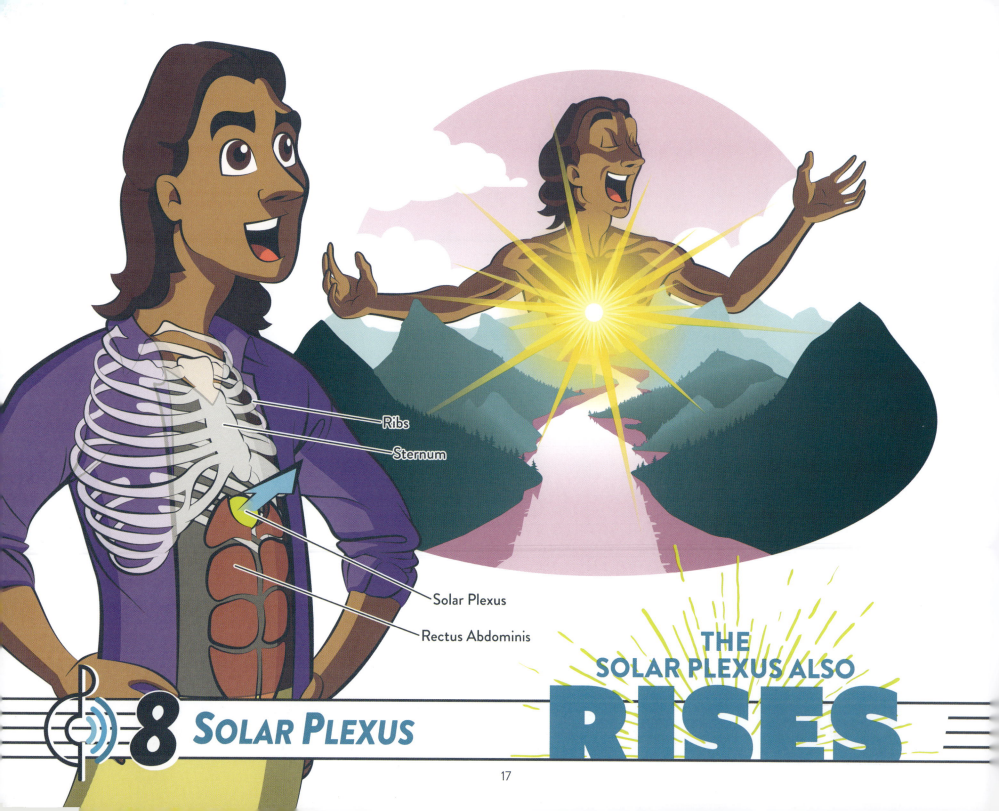

**MOST OF US LONG TO HAVE OUR... MOMENT IN THE SUN**

But, maybe the **SUN** should have its **MOMENT IN US!** After all, the sun is made of a heck of a lot of hydrogen, and so are we. In that sense, every single note you sing shines the sun's radiance back from whence it came. So, it's no surprise that some of singing's greatest "Star Power" originates from the **SOLAR PLEXUS**.

---

The **SOLAR PLEXUS** (celiac plexus) is a grouping of nerves located behind the upper abdominal muscles just below the sternum. *Solar* means "relating to the sun." *Plexus* means "network of nerves." So, the solar plexus can be thought of as a "sunshiny network of nerves!" All these nerves make the solar plexus a very sensitive area. For example, if you've ever had the wind knocked out of you, then you've definitely experienced this sensitivity! So, be sure to press gently when you locate this area with your hands.

The solar plexus plays a critical role not just in singing, but also in many of our everyday tasks via the Valsalva maneuver. The *Valsalva maneuver* occurs when breath pressure is pushed against closed vocal folds. You can experience this by making a sort of "heaving grunt" sound. The purpose of the Valsalva maneuver is to elevate the heart rate in order to assist with tasks such as coughing, lifting heavy objects, or using the bathroom. Valsalva maneuver pressure is typically created by squeezing the upper abdominals and solar plexus region to push breath against closed vocal folds. As a result, your vocal folds already know how to hold back great amounts of breath pressure.

Unfortunately, singing requires our vocal folds to hold back breath pressure a *teensy bit*, even though the Valsalva maneuver has already taught them to hold it back a lot. Therefore, we must be vigilant that the solar plexus never gets tight or rigid during singing. Any rigidity practically guarantees that the Valsalva maneuver is hindering our vocal freedom.

For practice, try your hiss once again. This time keep your fingers pressed into the solar plexus. As you inhale, you should notice that the solar plexus expands. As you exhale to hiss, make sure that the solar plexus also rises. Don't force it out—even a very small amount of rising is fine. If it doesn't rise for you, then it should at least stay pillowy and soft. The ultimate goal is to keep this area free from clenching and gripping as you sing. So, whenever you practice, simply remind this area to remain relaxed and radiant.

**To sing like never before**, the solar plexus must not be eclipsed by upper abdominal tension. Remember—*when your solar plexus glows, your singing flows*. So, salute the sun! After all, you've always been a star... LITERALLY!

---

**SLNB QUICK TIPS**

**1** Find your solar plexus by gently pressing into the upper abdominal area below your sternum.

**2** Squeeze your upper abs firmly and notice the effect this has on your breath and vocal folds.

**3** Practice keeping your solar plexus region as soft and expansive as you can while singing.

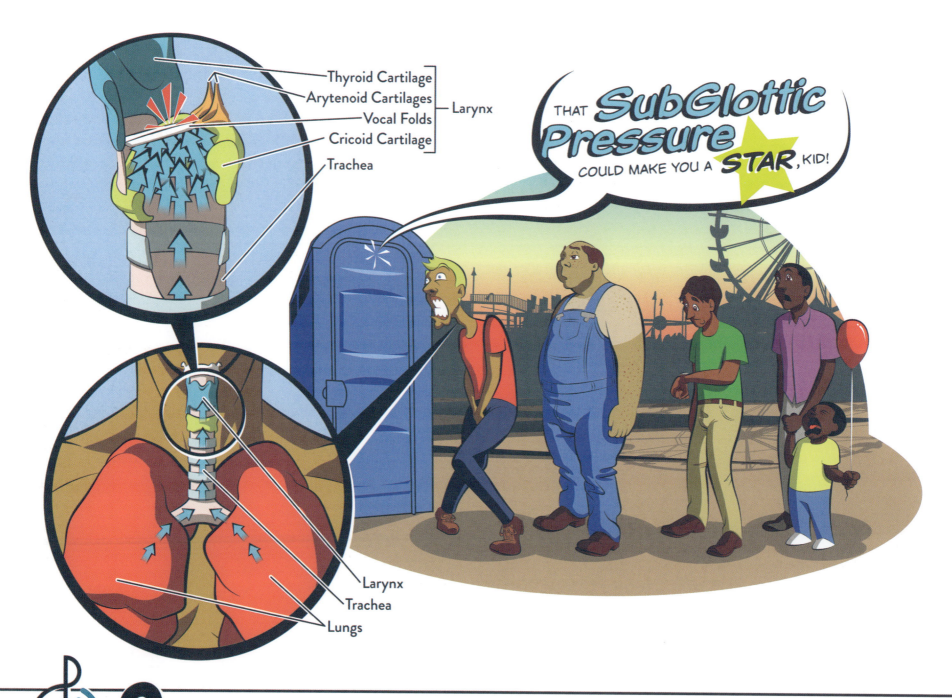

| You are waiting for the only restroom within a hundred miles. That's why... | You've been patiently holding your breath and biting your tongue because you have no choice... | You feel like SCREAMING but your politeness forces you... | YOU ARE BURSTING WITH LIQUID RAGE |
|---|---|---|---|
| YOU'VE GOT TO HOLD IT IN. | YOU'VE GOT TO HOLD IT IN! | TO HOLD IT IN! | WITH SUBGLOTTIC PRESSURE! |

**SUBGLOTTIC PRESSURE** is breath pressure that builds up beneath the vocal folds when they are closed. "Sub" means "below." "Glottic" refers to the *glottis*, which is the space between the vocal folds. So, subglottic pressure is a rather fancy way of describing breath that's essentially trapped in the lungs. To experience subglottic pressure, try holding your breath for a few seconds with your vocal folds pressed together.

Subglottic pressure differs from "lung volume" and "airflow." *Lung volume* is the quantity of breath in the lungs. *Airflow* is the breath's ability to pass from the lungs through the vocal tract. Subglottic pressure, though, is the potential created by air in the lungs as it interacts with the vocal folds. In singing, this *potential* results in two primary outcomes: pitch and volume.

### PITCH

To produce pitch, the vocal folds need airflow to set them into vibration. Vibrations are faster for higher notes and slower for lower notes. That's why it's instinctive for us to use more air to achieve higher notes. Unfortunately, this is also one of our most costly habits as more air is not necessarily required to make the vocal folds vibrate faster. With this habit, we end up with unnecessarily large inhalations, excessive subglottic pressure, and the tendency to "push" with forceful exhalations. As you practice, make sure that you don't take and use needless amounts of breath to achieve higher notes. Instead, use a small and steady airflow to ensure that your pitch doesn't rely too heavily on force, pressure, and loudness.

### VOLUME

As subglottic pressure increases, the potential for louder vocal sounds also increases. Granted, volume isn't created by breath alone. Breath must also interact with vocal fold compression and the shape of the vocal tract. Ultimately though, learning to regulate subglottic pressure is a key element for achieving volume control and dynamics. As you practice, notice the connection your breath has to your volume. Find the most comfortable volume for any given note that you sing. Then, see if you can both decrescendo (get softer) and crescendo (get louder) using breath as your primary source for the volume change.

**To sing like never before**, you don't have to hold it in any longer. After all, too much subglottic pressure can only make your singing sound like it could BURST at any moment. On the other hand, subglottic pressure that is well managed with breath support will help you control pitch and volume. So, go ahead and breathe a sigh of relief. It's finally your turn...

 **SLNB QUICK TIPS**

**1** Experience subglottic pressure by holding your breath with your vocal folds together.

**2** As you sing throughout your range, see how steady you can keep your breath pressure.

**3** Try singing at different volume levels and observe the connection this has to your breathing.

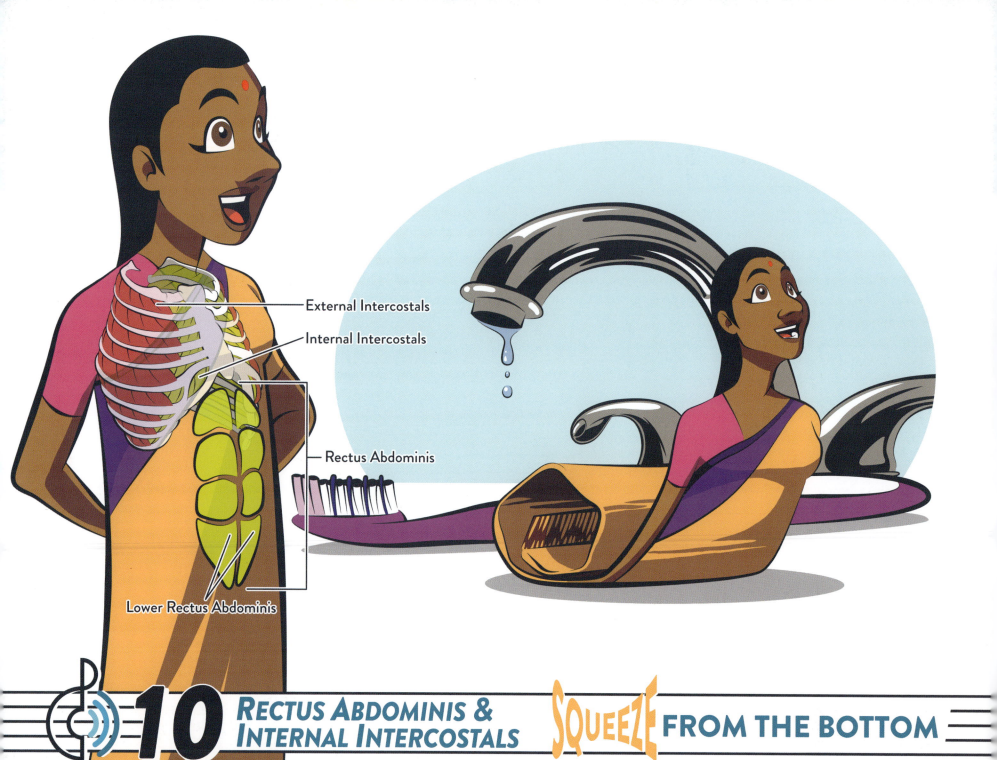

**If you squeeze your toothpaste from the top, you won't get any paste.**

**If you squeeze from the middle, you'll get a monumental mess of flowing fluoride!**

**If you squeeze from the bottom - what will you get?**

**OPTIMAL TOOTHPASTE EFFICIENCY!**

Interestingly, optimal singing works much the same way. We've learned that breath support essentially means "resist the exhale." Yet, we still must exhale somehow, or else we'll never sing! So, let's explore some muscles that *should* engage when we exhale.

The **RECTUS ABDOMINIS** is an abdominal muscle that brings the chest and pelvis toward each other. It's perhaps better known as the "six-pack muscle," as it also firms and flexes the abdomen. Along with the transverse abdominis, the rectus abdominis has the potential to expel breath quickly by flattening the belly. However, fast and forceful exhales don't make for good breath support, or for efficient singing.

Thankfully, we can actually engage various cans of the six pack at our liberty. In other words, we can control individual sections of the rectus abdominis. Since the lower rectus abdominis is the lowest point of engagement in all of the breathing musculature, an extremely gentle engagement of these muscles offers the greatest mechanical advantage. This maximizes our ability to release air in a slow, consistent, and controlled fashion.

The *internal intercostals* are muscles that run between each rib and close the rib cage during exhalation. Holding the rib cage open at all times causes rigidity in the breathing system and the body. Meanwhile, aggressive downward thrusting of the upper body is the antithesis of breath support. The internal intercostals help balance these two extremes by allowing the ribs to descend gradually, with the lowest ribs leading the way.

Ideally, we want the rectus abdominis and the internal intercostals to work in harmony during exhalations. The final product should eventually become automatic, and often feels quite subtle. So subtle, in fact, that some singers may even feel as though the diaphragm is simply rising with very little assistance of any kind. This feeling might be described as energetic, but never forceful. Or, perhaps relaxed, but never passive.

**To sing like never before**, you don't have to fight tooth and nail. You just need to "squeeze from the bottom!" That is, your exhalations should very subtly and naturally initiate from the lowest and most advantageous points in your breathing system. You brush every day without even thinking about it. When your breathing technique becomes this automatic, you have no choice except to... SMILE!

**1** Practice subtly engaging the lowest point in your abdomen with a hiss or a lightly sung phrase.

**2** Allow your rib cage to descend gradually and evenly as you practice breathing and singing.

**3** Like in appoggio breathing, try combining these gestures for balanced and controlled exhales.

# CHAPTER 2
*THE LARYNX*

# THERE'S AN ELEPHANT IN THE ROOM!

## BUT THIS ELEPHANT DOESN'T HAVE... ENORMOUS EARS, A GARGANTUAN GIRTH OR A STUPENDOUS SNOUT

In fact, this elusive elephant is the vocal instrument *itself*. Surprisingly, singers and even voice teachers often overlook this elephant entirely. **WHAT A MAMMOTH MISTAKE!** After all, pianists don't close the piano and practice on the lid. Guitarists don't remove all the strings and say: "Let's **ROCK!**" Flutists don't grab a straw and simply hope for the best. Nope—they master their *instruments*! Similarly, singers must never neglect their own instrument—the **LARYNX**.

---

The **LARYNX** is made up of a singular bone and a grouping of cartilages in the neck that form the vocal apparatus and house the vocal folds. This minuscule mechanism is roughly the size of a golf ball. Yet, it has the potential to produce practically every vocal sound known to mankind. If you've never located your larynx, it's time to finally find the elephant in the room!

Place a finger on your chin. Slide it down the underside of your chin toward the middle of your neck. You should notice a small protuberance if you're a female, or a larger one if you're a male. This is the thyroid cartilage—the largest structure in the larynx. Once you've found it, keep your finger there and try swallowing. You should notice that your larynx leaps! Next, try yawning. Your larynx drops down!

The larynx is the only free-floating structure in the skeletal system. The only thing that comes close to its range of motion is the patella (knee cap). The larynx's suspensory nature gives it maximal mobility. This is part of what allows the larynx to participate in several essential functions:

**BREATHING**—the larynx helps regulate breath as it travels in and out of the body.

**SWALLOWING**—the larynx lifts and seals off the airway so that food and liquids don't get into the lungs.

**YAWNING**—the larynx drops and opens so that greater quantities of oxygen can enter the lungs.

**SPEECH AND SINGING**—the larynx moves freely between its highest and lowest positions to accommodate air as it passes through to set the vocal folds into vibration.

**To sing like never before**, we must no longer overlook the larynx as our vocal instrument. Understanding and mastering its nuances is fundamental for vocal technique. It's actually so obvious that not even an elephant could forget it! He who has ears, let him hear...

---

 Don't be afraid of your larynx! Make sure to locate its position and feel it with your fingers.

 Try yawning and swallowing to observe the ways that the larynx can move between extremes.

 As you sing, start to become aware of which situations cause your larynx to rise or to fall.

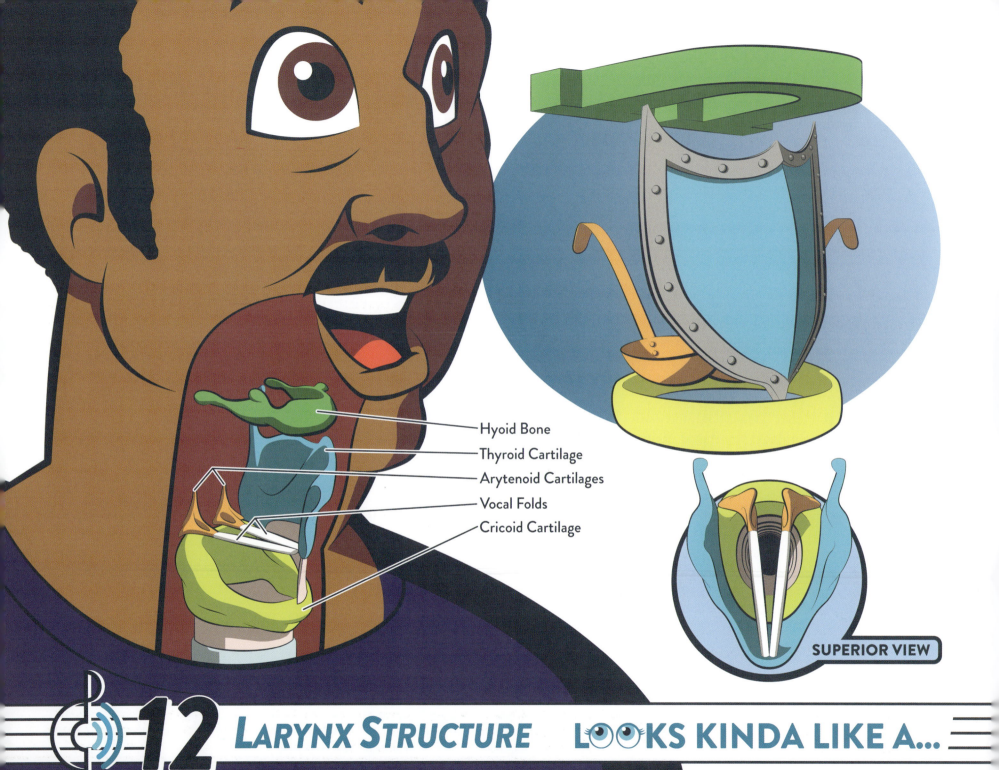

| WHAT IF YOUR DOCTOR ASKED YOU TO... | WHAT IF HE THEN ASKED TO... | OR, WHAT IF SHE WANTED YOU TO... | This would be unimaginably simplistic anatomy! Yet, when it comes to larynx structure — |
|---|---|---|---|
| TAKE A DEEP BREATH INTO THOSE "ACCORDION-LOOKIN' THINGS"  | PEEK INSIDE YOUR "FLAPPY SOUND HOLES"  | OPEN UP YOUR "FOOD CAVE" AND STICK OUT YOUR "SLIMY RED TASTE-TESTER"  | IT LOOKS KINDA LIKE THAT'S WHAT WE'VE GOT!  |

**THE LARYNX'S STRUCTURE** consists of three primary cartilages and one bone. All of the larynx's primary structures end with the suffix "oid," which roughly translates to "looks kinda like." The prefixes like "hy-," "crico-," "thyro-," and "aryten-" refer to common shapes and everyday objects. So, the larynx's primary parts shouldn't be daunting. After all, they get their names simply because they "look kinda like" something.

**HYOID BONE**
The hyoid bone "looks kinda like the letter U" and is the larynx's only bone. It's also the only free-floating bone in the body, as it is not attached to any other bone. This is what gives the larynx its tremendous range of motion for yawning, swallowing, and adopting the many different positions required for speech and singing.

**THYROID CARTILAGE**
The thyroid cartilage "looks kinda like a shield" at the front of the larynx. The vocal folds attach to the back of the thyroid and are protected by its shielding. The thyroid is also called the Adam's apple, and is more pronounced in men than it is in women.

**CRICOID CARTILAGE**
The cricoid cartilage "looks kinda like a ring" at the base of the larynx. It's situated at the top of the trachea. The trachea is the windpipe which allows air to flow between the larynx and the lungs. The cricoid serves as the gateway between the larynx and the trachea.

**ARYTENOID CARTILAGES**
The arytenoid cartilages "look kinda like soup ladles" sitting atop the cricoid. The vocal folds attach to the arytenoids at the larynx's posterior and to the thyroid at the larynx's anterior. Just like the hyoid bone, the arytenoids possess an impressive range of motion. They can move side to side, front to back, and also rotate inward and outward. This dynamic range of motion accommodates the spectacular spectrum of sounds that singers can make.

**To sing like never before**, it's important that we understand the structure of our vocal instrument. However, anatomy doesn't need to be intimidating. Instead, it looks kinda like we can just call it like we see it!

 **① Don't be intimidated by anatomy. Instead, challenge yourself to understand your instrument!** **② Larynx parts are named after common objects like a "U," a shield, a ring, or soup ladles.** **③ Locate your hyoid, cricoid, and thyroid with your fingers. (Sorry, arytenoids are on the inside.)**

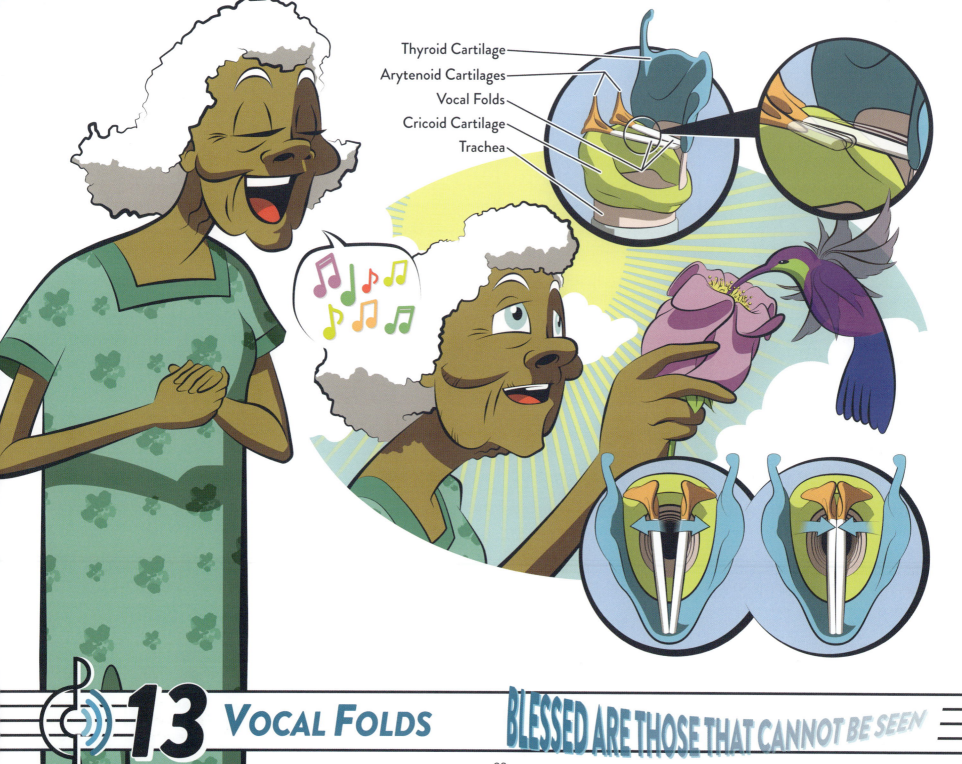

Have you ever experienced the Joy of seeing a hummingbird?

If you have, then you've stumbled upon something divine—feeble wings flapping furiously for a farfetched feat of flight! The human eye is left in helpless awe, incapable of witnessing these weariless wings working. And so it is with many of life's most minuscule miracles. Amidst the chaos, the noise, and the flash—True Beauty often goes unseen.

The Vocal Folds understand this plight as well as any other instigator of inspiration. And still—they insist on moving faster than the eye can see. It's almost as if they are conscious that their diminutive size possesses the ability to say, "I  you," to leave an audience in tears, or even to change the world.

---

The **VOCAL FOLDS** are two mucous membrane tissues within the larynx that are capable of rapid vibrations faster than the human eye can perceive. These vibrations produce the sound waves that create the human voice. The vocal folds are only as long as your pinky nail (usually 12-25 mm). Yet, their small size is no hindrance to their numerous anatomic and vocal abilities.

Anatomically, the vocal folds have two primary tasks. The first is to prevent foods and liquids from entering the trachea and lungs if they've somehow managed to sneak past the epiglottis. The second is to hold air in the body via the Valsalva maneuver. This assists with activities such as lifting heavy objects, going to the bathroom, and coughing.

In singing and speech, the vocal folds create sound via the mucosal wave. The mucosal wave is the vibratory cycle of the vocal folds during phonation. In other words, they separate and come back together in a wave-like way. To put this in perspective, a hummingbird's wings flap about seventy times per second. To the vocal folds, that's nothing. They vibrate hundreds and even thousands of times per second!

As air passes through the larynx, the vocal folds have the ability to abduct (open) and to adduct (close). When they are fully abducted, air can pass through them freely. When they are fully adducted, air is restricted from passing in or out. However, when they are adducted with balance and moderation, the result is a most miraculous movement. The vocal folds are set into rapid vibration by the air, and the voice takes flight!

**To sing like never before**, we must appreciate that the smallest things in life often produce the greatest beauty. Humble wings lift the hummingbird. Humble folds lift the singer. Humble singing lifts the soul. All without ever being seen.

---

## SLNB QUICK TIPS

**1** Examine your pinky nail. This is the approximate size of the vocal folds within your larynx.

**2** As you sing, notice the vibrations in your neck and larynx. Those are your vocal folds at work!

**3** Consider things in your life that cannot be seen, but nevertheless produce breathtaking beauty.

**FLUFFY'S** MASTER WORKS HARD SO THAT FLUFFY CAN HAVE A BETTER LIFE.

Fluffy would never deign to accept anything less than his **CAVIAR-FLAVORED CAT FOOD**, his **IMPORTED DESIGNER CATNIP**, and *especially* his **CUSTOM-MADE MULTI-LAYERED LUXURY CAT BED**

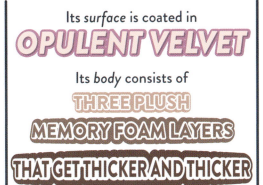

Its *surface* is coated in **OPULENT VELVET**. Its *body* consists of **THREE PLUSH MEMORY FOAM LAYERS THAT GET THICKER AND THICKER**

Its *base* even has a switch that can change the bed's firmness. So, anytime Fluffy curls up for his catnap, he rests knowing that this level of sophistication has never been rivaled.

**OR HAS IT?**

---

The **VOCAL FOLD LAYERS** are an incredibly sophisticated design consisting of the epithelium, lamina propria, and the thyroarytenoid muscle. The epithelium is the surface of the vocal folds. Three layers of lamina propria make up their interior. The deepest layer is the thyroarytenoid muscle. Let's explore each one!

## SURFACE

The epithelium is the outermost layer and structural surface of the vocal folds. Try taking your tongue and gliding it across the inside of your cheek. The surface of your inner cheek is quite comparable to the epithelium. The epithelium is similarly moist, soft, and flexible, yet solid enough to provide shape and structure to the vocal folds. Beneath the epithelium is the lamina propria.

## INTERIOR

The lamina propria is the vibratory interior of the vocal folds. It's divided into three mucosal layers: the superficial, the intermediate, and the deep layer. Each layer is composed of fibers that get progressively thicker and more viscous. This provides a cushion-like protection for the vocal folds.

The superficial lamina propria has the least thickness and therefore vibrates the most easily. The intermediate lamina propria is more viscous, and the deep lamina propria layer is thicker still. The deeper layers are there to provide more protection and structural integrity for the vocal folds. Thus, they do not vibrate as easily or as freely as the outer layer. As we move up in pitch, the vocal folds thin out, so that less thickness and mass are used for higher notes.

## MUSCLE

The deepest layer of the vocal folds consists of muscle. The thyroarytenoid muscle shortens and also flexes the vocal folds. It is the only vocal muscle that is actually *inside* the folds. Other muscles that control our voices influence the folds in several ways. However, singing is largely made possible thanks to the fact that we have this muscular control built into our vocal folds. We'll look at how this works in the next section!

**To sing like never before**, we must take a tip from Fluffy: if you're going to live nine lives, then you'd better have a great bed. Similarly, if your folds are going to vibrate billions of times throughout your life, then you'd better have vocal fold layers. With their flexible coating, multilayered vibrational capabilities, protective cushioning, and internal muscular control, it's almost as if your vocal folds were designed with royalty in mind!

---

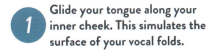
Glide your tongue along your inner cheek. This simulates the surface of your vocal folds.

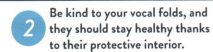
Be kind to your vocal folds, and they should stay healthy thanks to their protective interior.

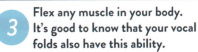
Flex any muscle in your body. It's good to know that your vocal folds also have this ability.

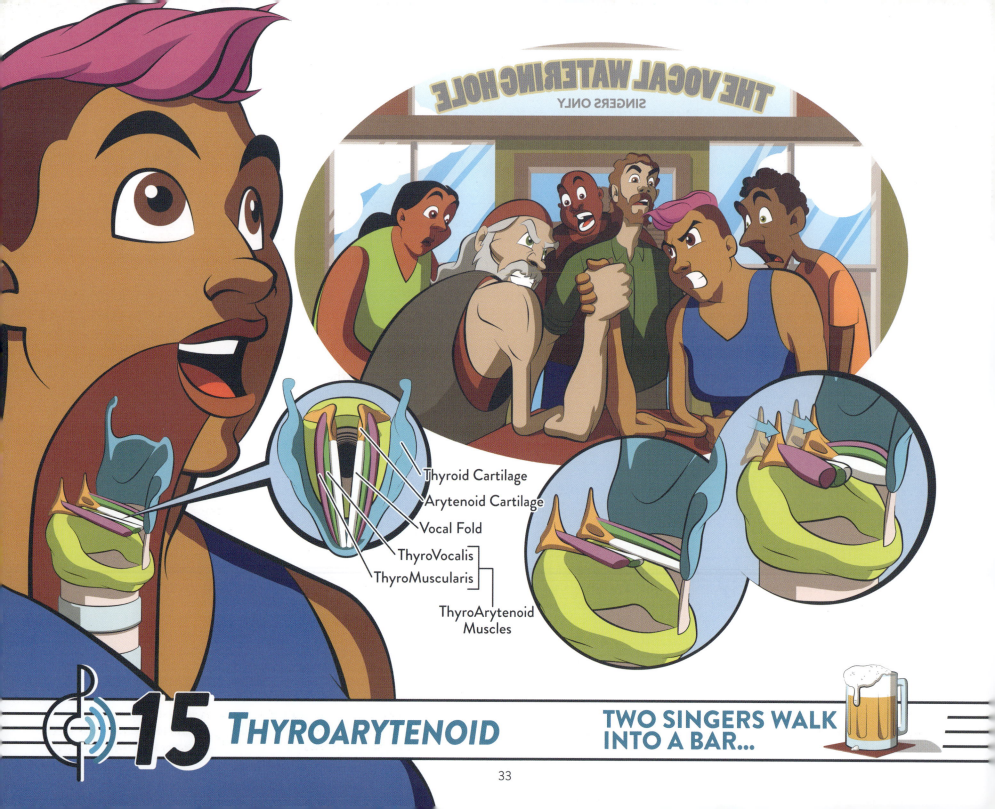

## STOP ME IF YOU'VE HEARD THIS ONE:

Two singers walk into a bar and get into an arm-wrestling contest. As their hands meet, both singers *forfeit* and the match is instantly called a draw. Why? Because they realize that they completely forgot to **BUILD THEIR BICEPS!!!** They spent all their time training their **THYROARYTENOIDS!**

The **THYROARYTENOID** (TA) is the larynx muscle responsible for shortening and thickening the vocal folds. "Thyroarytenoid" may seem like an intimidating term initially, but it's actually just what it sounds like: thyro(id)-arytenoid. It attaches to the thyroid cartilage in the front, and to each arytenoid cartilage in the back. Its actions bring the arytenoid cartilages nearer to the thyroid cartilage, shortening the folds. This all actually happens *inside* the vocal folds, as the TA is their deepest layer. Interestingly, its muscular actions work similarly in many ways to the biceps.

So, let's see those guns! Stretch your arm straight out in front of you. From there, don't move your arm, but simply flex your biceps. Notice that you can flex your biceps without your arm moving. Next, bring your hand to your shoulder. Notice that you don't have to flex your biceps in order to do it. Instead, you have a choice on exactly how much to shorten your arm or how much to flex your arm. This is because your biceps can perform *two actions*. In fact, that's why they're called bi (two)—ceps (heads). One action makes the muscle shorter, and the other action makes the muscle firmer—just like the thyroarytenoid.

The shortening element of the TA (known as the thyromuscularis) is primarily responsible for lowering the pitch when we sing. Shorter vocal folds are bulkier and looser. Therefore, they vibrate more slowly as breath passes through them. Slower vibrations result in lower pitches, while faster vibrations result in higher pitches.

The firming element of the TA (known as the thyrovocalis) is primarily responsible for strengthening the tone when we sing. The more flexed the vocal folds are, the better they are at resisting the breath. The result is a stronger, more solid, and sometimes louder sound that is capable of a broader spectrum or resonance.

**To sing like never before**, toning up the biceps is optional. But, toning up the TA is a must. Anytime your sound gets stronger or your pitch gets lower, it's fairly safe to say that your thyroarytenoids are getting a workout. So, set the bar high when it comes to exercising your voice. If you do, your vocal muscles will be "no joke!"

 **1** Try singing in the lower part of your range. Your thyroarytenoid is shortening your vocal folds. **2** Speak or sing in a very powerful voice. Your thyroarytenoid is flexing your vocal folds. **3** Practice singing at different levels of intensity. Do you notice any change coming from within?

 **Q: HOW DO I SING A HIGH NOTE?**

 **Q: WHAT THE HECK DOES THAT MEAN?! DON'T I HAVE TO FIX MY BREATHING? PLACE THE SOUND IN THE MASQUE? OPEN MY MOUTH WIDER? LIFT MY EYEBROWS? SQUEEZE MY BUTT CHEEKS?**

 **A: JUST USE YOUR CRICOTHYROID!**

**A: WELL...YOU COULD TRY THOSE THINGS. BUT, ALL YOU REALLY NEED IS YOUR**

The **CRICOTHYROID** (CT) is a larynx muscle that elevates vocal pitch by bringing the thyroid cartilage and cricoid cartilage nearer together. This causes the vocal folds to stretch out and lengthen. Long, thin, taut vocal folds vibrate more quickly than short, bulky, loose vocal folds. Faster vibrations create high notes!

**QUESTION:** "But isn't it bad to sing from the larynx?"

**ANSWER:** "Actually, it's the ONLY way to sing!"

The larynx can do more than just move up and down. It can actually move from *within*. The cricothyroid joint is the pivot point inside the larynx that allows the cricoid and thyroid cartilages to be repositioned or moved together. This movement happens when you use your CT muscle. Another name for this is "laryngeal tilt." If it weren't for your larynx's ability to move like this, you wouldn't be able to stretch your vocal folds for high notes.

**QUESTION:** "But how will I know when I've engaged my CT?"

**ANSWER:** "When your voice, your larynx, and your body feel relaxed and yet you just happen to be singing higher!"

The cricothyroid is the voice's best answer to straining. So, if you're struggling with high notes, here are some questions for you. Are you: *Pushing air and volume? Squeezing the larynx? Tightening the neck? Gripping the jaw? Tensing the tongue? Widening the mouth?* All of these habits can potentially lessen the voice's reliance on the cricothyroid. On the other hand, anytime the body stays calm and the pitch still goes higher—that's when the CT is doing its job without any outside assistance!

As you practice, notice what sensations you feel as you move up and down throughout your range. Many singers have the experience of their sound traveling up and back as pitches go higher. It's common for higher notes to feel like they're moving toward the crown of the head. If you feel this sensation, then this is another sign that your CT is at work!

**To sing like never before**, going higher comes down to the cricothyroid muscle. If high notes have to answer to the CT, then they will certainly succeed. No question about it!

---

  **1** As you sing higher, feel how the sound travels up and back. That's your CT muscle at work!

 **2** To improve your technique, maximize the use of the CT muscle by minimizing vocal strain.

 **3** You'll know that your voice is relying on the CT muscle when high notes feel relaxed and easy.

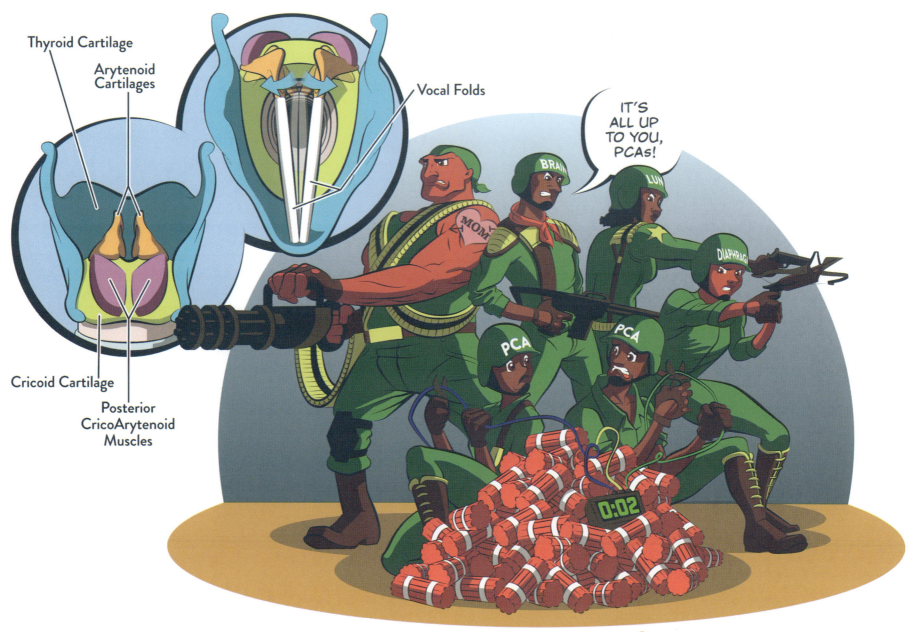

**17 POSTERIOR CRICOARYTENOIDS** — THE UNSUNG HEROES

DID YOU EVER CONSIDER THAT YOUR VOICE COULD SAVE YOUR LIFE?

OUR HEARTS HEROICALLY HAUL BLOOD

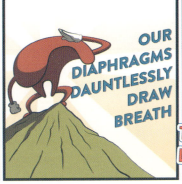
OUR DIAPHRAGMS DAUNTLESSLY DRAW BREATH

OUR BRAINS BRAVELY BELLOW COMMANDS
THEY'RE A LITANY OF LITERAL LIFE-SAVERS!

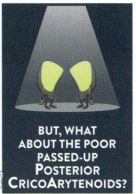
BUT, WHAT ABOUT THE POOR PASSED-UP POSTERIOR CRICOARYTENOIDS?

The **POSTERIOR CRICOARYTENOIDS** (PCAs) are the larynx muscles exclusively responsible for opening the vocal folds. When the vocal folds are shut, air cannot travel in or out of the lungs. When the vocal folds are open, air can move freely.

The PCAs attach to the backs of both the cricoid cartilage and the arytenoid cartilages. When they contract, the backs of the arytenoids spin inward and their front sides spin outward. This spinning action opens the vocal folds.

Every breath that we take involves the PCAs. So, a lot depends upon their success. If they should somehow fail their mission, our demise would be asphyxiation and suffocation. Thankfully, it's exceedingly rare for the PCAs to fall in battle!

Aside from saving your life, the PCAs can also help you achieve lighter vocal productions and breathier (aspirate) qualities. The vocal folds have to come together to make sound. However, excessive compression often results in pressed, squeezed, or even raspy qualities. The more the PCAs are engaged, the less contact the vocal folds make. Thus, the PCAs serve as antagonists to the compression and adduction muscles.

You can discover this by using the glottic consonant H. Glottic consonants are consonants that occur at the level of the vocal folds (glottis). During any H, the vocal folds are moved apart by the PCAs. Entering into any sound through an H helps to reduce excessive compression on the vocal folds and achieve softer and gentler vocal qualities.

You can also try speaking in a breathy voice. If you've never done this before, you'll find it somewhere in between a whisper and your normal voice. Start by gently speaking the phrase "breathy voice" while letting a very small bit of air get past your vocal folds. Once you've established a gentle and easy breathy sound in your speaking voice, experiment with it in your singing. When you do, it's very important to know that *you don't need to use a lot of air*. Not only can this be a bit drying to the vocal folds, but it will also cause you to run out of air very quickly. So, whenever you use breathy qualities: save your breath and let your PCAs take charge instead!

**To sing like never before**, let's salute the larynx muscles that keep us alive without ever even making a sound. They are truly our unSUNG heroes. Were it not for the PCAs—our breath would be MIA!

**SLNB QUICK TIPS**

**1** Inhale and exhale. Your PCAs open your vocal folds to allow air to flow through your larynx.

**2** If your voice is too squeezed or compressed, try initiating sounds with the glottic consonant H.

**3** Speak or sing in a breathy (aspirate) voice to experience the PCAs at work during phonation.

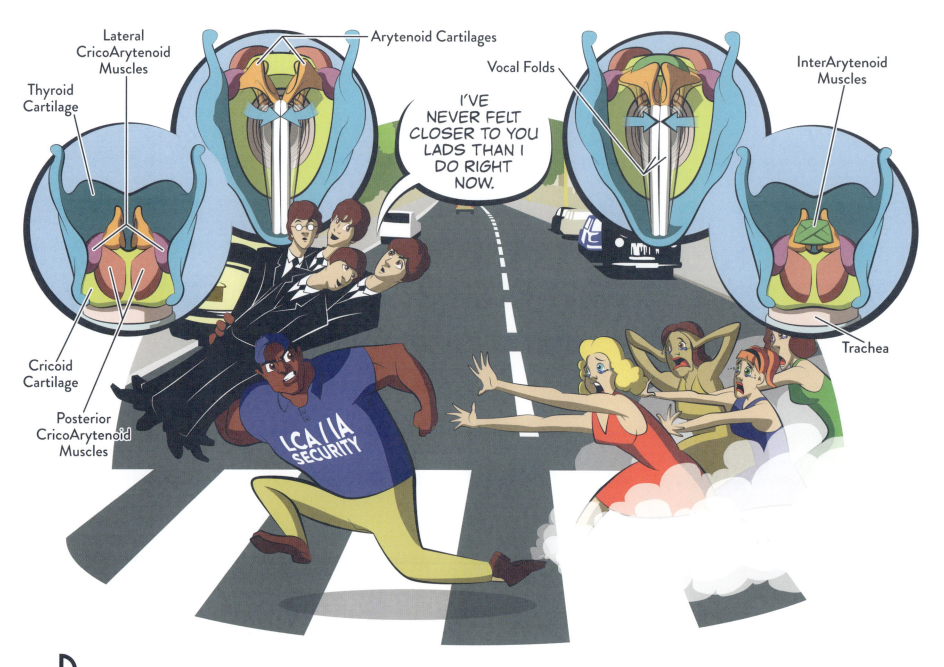

In this **HELTER SKELTER** day and age, singing might just be the best way to **give peace a chance.**  We say we **WANT A REVOLUTION** When **all we** really **need is love.** Just **IMAGINE ALL THE PEOPLE** singing for a tomorrow that's better than **YESTERDAY.** This path to peace may be a **long and winding road.** But, we can **WORK IT OUT** with **a little help from our friends**... **THE VOCAL FOLDS!** They must **COME TOGETHER... RIGHT NOW...**

The **LATERAL CRICOARYTENOIDS** (LCAs) and **INTERARYTENOIDS** (IAs) are the two primary larynx muscles responsible for the vocal folds coming together. Vocal fold closure (also called "compression" or "adduction") is necessary for producing all voiced sounds in both singing and speech. In fact, if you've ever found yourself speaking words of wisdom or singing in the dead of night, then it's a guarantee these muscles have both been working like a dog.

The lateral cricoarytenoids are situated on the sides (laterals) of the larynx and run between the cricoid cartilage and arytenoid cartilages. When they contract, the arytenoids spin inward, causing the vocal folds to come together.

The interarytenoids are exactly what they sound like—the muscles located in between (inter) the arytenoids. The IAs bring the arytenoids nearer to each other, which also causes the vocal folds to come together.

Vocal fold closure from the LCAs and IAs is perhaps best experienced through the use of glottals. Glottals are clicking sounds created by the articulation of the vocal folds. They generally occur at the onset of words that begin with vowels. Try saying the phrase "uh oh!" and notice the clicking that happens. This is your vocal folds pressing together before the vibration begins for each vowel sound. These are glottals!

Glottals can be a very effective tool for encouraging vocal fold closure. They are particularly helpful for singers whose sound is consistently too breathy (aspirate). If this is the case for you, then try singing on a vowel sound and begin with a gentle, but intentional glottal. Try to maintain some of the feeling of the glottal closure as you sing the vowel. This should very quickly help you to gain access to a crisper and cleaner sound.

Just like any muscle, the LCAs and IAs can be taught various degrees of control. So, using them too much or too aggressively may cause a squeezed or pressed sound. However, not using them enough may cause a weak or breathy sound. Experiment with your voice to make sure that you can find a sound that is not too pressed or too breathy. Once you've got the hang of it, you'll have found your ideal balance of vocal fold closure!

**To sing like never before**, take a sad song and make it better! In other words, make sure that your vocal folds know how to come together. In the end, the sounds you awake are equal to the vocal fold contact... you make...

  If your voice feels too weak or breathy, then you'll need to increase your vocal fold closure.  Try using glottals to experience more vocal fold closure from your LCA and IA muscles.  Experiment as you practice to find a neutral sound that is neither too breathy nor too pressed.

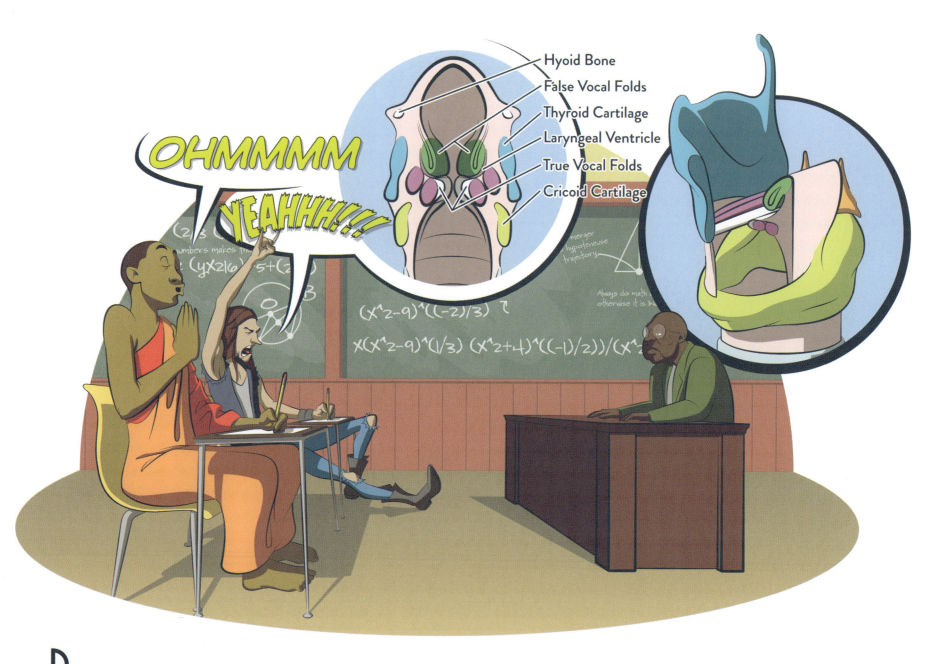

 The vocal folds must vibrate for the larynx to make a sound.
☐ TRUE
☒ FALSE

 There is only one pair of vocal folds.
☐ TRUE
☒ FALSE

 This quiz is clearly making up falsehoods about the vocal folds.
☐ TRUE
☒ FALSE!

The **FALSE VOCAL FOLDS** are located just above the "true" vocal folds and provide auxiliary closure and vibration within the larynx. They're also called the vestibular folds, or ventricular folds. "Vestibule" and "ventricle" are terms that refer to chambers or spaces. So, these names derive from the fact that the false vocal folds hang down above the true vocal folds, creating small chambers above them.

Vocal folds are generally used when ultra-firm closure of the larynx is required, like during a cough or grunt. Such closure also helps prevent choking by keeping food and liquid out of the trachea. Also, the false vocal folds assist with elevating subglottic pressure for some physical tasks like the Valsalva maneuver. With all of this true-blue reliability, isn't it quizzical that the false vocal folds are still referred to as "false"?

We learned that the true vocal folds are incredibly sophisticated due to their five facets—the epithelium, lamina propria layers, and muscle. In stark contrast, the false vocal folds are just two fleshy flaps (mucous membranes). Bringing them together does not produce a vast variety of vibrations. Instead, they produce a remarkable racket of rasp.

Some vocal styles feature these rasp and distortion qualities quite frequently. Examples include certain world styles like Tibetan Buddhist chanting, and several contemporary styles like rock and heavy metal. This said, most vocal styles use the false vocal folds quite sparingly, and they are mainly needed for occasions that require their distorted qualities. So, most singers will rarely use their false vocal folds.

If you do want to use your false vocal folds, the simplest way to begin to experience them is by clearing your throat. Of course, aggressive throat clearing isn't good for the voice, but it's just fine if done lightly and moderately. Start by clearing your throat in a very gentle way. Then, try humming simultaneously for a few seconds. Your false vocal folds will vibrate, and your arytenoid cartilages will rattle too. You should hear a dramatic, yet effortless raspy vibration. If so, then you've discovered your false vocal folds!

**To sing like never before**, we need to take a true or false quiz when it comes to the larynx. If we do, then we'll truly understand any falsehoods about the true vocal folds, and the truth about the false vocal folds... uhhhhh...**TRUE!**

**Disclaimer:** Always exercise caution when experimenting with all distortion varieties. Pain and hoarseness are not okay. Study with a distortion specialist for mastery of the skills introduced in this section.

① The false vocal folds are used most frequently for vocal styles requiring rasp and distortion.

② You don't need to use your false vocal folds. Most singers use them sparingly or not at all.

③ If you'd like to begin finding your false vocal folds, try humming through a gentle throat clear.

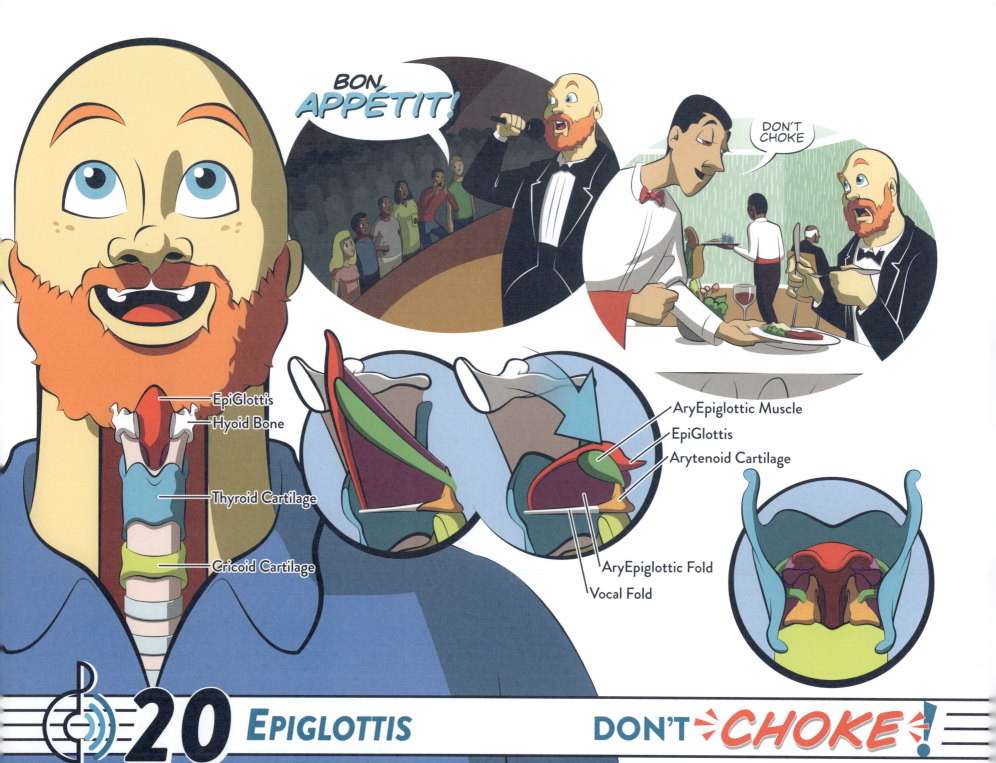

Before we take the stage to sing, it seems like there's always some well-meaning soul who yells out:

# DON'T CHOKE!

While this might be quite rude, it's actually fairly decent advice. After all, our stomachs are meant for food and our lungs are meant for air. It's never supposed to be the other way around. So what exactly happened when we sat down to a pleasant meal only to find ourselves blue-faced and **CHOKING?** Our **EPIGLOTTIS** literally took a lunch break!

---

The **EPIGLOTTIS** is a leaf-shaped cartilage that folds over the top of the larynx to prevent foods, liquids, and foreign objects from entering the lungs. The prefix "epi-" means "above." "Glottis" refers to the vocal folds and the space between them. So, the epiglottis gets its name simply from its convenient location *above* the vocal folds.

Location is everything! Especially for a cartilage designed to prevent things from lodging themselves between the vocal folds. All the epiglottis has to do is simply fold down, and objects are instantly delivered into the esophagus instead of the trachea. And when it fails to do so? Yep… it choked.

Other than preventing physical choking, can the epiglottis help us not to "choke" as singers as well? Absolutely! In fact, the epiglottic area (supraglottis) plays an important supporting role in boosting the voice's brightness. When the epiglottis is pushed backwards, or the space above the vocal folds is narrowed, it often results in a brighter resonance and tone.

Give it a try! Speak the phrase "TWANGY VOICE" in your most bratty, brassy, and nasty character voice. You may feel some movement at the base of your tongue when making this sound. You might also experience the sensation of your larynx lifting, or your throat becoming narrower or smaller. In either case, if your voice suddenly sounds bright and ringy, then you've successfully narrowed your vocal tract to create twang—bright resonances created by the epiglottis, larynx, and pharynx.

Narrower spaces like these bring out brighter resonances, while more cavernous spaces bring out darker resonances. Overusing bright qualities like twang makes the voice sound strident and cartoony. However, neglecting these qualities can leave the voice sounding dull and lifeless. As we will see in the next chapter, it's important to explore, balance, and fine-tune all of our resonance capabilities.

**To sing like never before**, it's always best if you don't choke! And that means the epiglottis must get down to business. Whether it's to send food into the right place or to brighten our singing voices, this cartilage goes "epi-" and beyond!

---

 **SLNB QUICK TIPS**

1. Aside from keeping you from choking, your epiglottic area helps add twang to your voice.

2. To discover twang, speak or sing in a bright, brassy, or piercing sounding character voice.

3. Include twang in your vocal resonance, but don't overdo it unless you want to sound cartoony.

# CHAPTER 3
*VOCAL RESONANCE & TONE*

## 21 SOUND — IT'S OUT OF THIS WORLD!

## LOOKING FOR SOME PEACE AND QUIET?

**How about the park?** — TOO MANY CHIRPING BIRDS!

**Okay, what about the library?** — TOO MANY FLIPPING PAGES!!

**Maybe try your closet?** — TOO MUCH ANNOYING BREATHING!!!

**Alright, fine! Why not just go to outer space?! There's TOTAL SILENCE in space. Absolutely… No.. Sound… Whatsoever!** — YES!

**SOUND** can be defined most simply as vibrations that travel through the air. These vibrations are also called "sound waves." Water and several other mediums can also carry sound waves. However, sound (as we usually know it) exists because of vibrating air and our ears' ability to perceive these vibrations. Since there's no air in outer space, there can also be no sound!

Thankfully though, there's an abundance of air right here on Earth. And plenty of otherworldly singing to be done as a result. But, if sound requires air vibrations, then we'd certainly better learn how to vibrate that air! Only three elements are required to do it: a power supply, a vibratory source, and resonance spaces.

### POWER SUPPLY

The power supply is our breath. Exhalations of varying degrees of speed and force bring air up from the lungs and through the larynx. As breath moves through the larynx, it begins to interact with the vocal folds. Greater breath pressure creates the potential for more power, whereas less breath pressure reduces this potential. Striking the ideal balance is a major goal for every singer.

### VIBRATORY SOURCE

The vibratory source is our vocal folds. This is where the actual sound-making takes place. The vocal folds "chop up" our breath into sonic bursts by rapidly opening and closing (vibrating) as air interacts with them inside the larynx. These vibrations create sound waves that are strengthened and enhanced by resonance when they bounce off of spaces inside our head. This is also called "resonance."

### RESONANCE SPACES

The resonance spaces are our pharynxes, mouths, and nasal cavities. These chambers amplify the sound waves created by our vocal folds and breath. Our vocal folds are quite tiny. So, their opening and closing alone doesn't result in very dynamic sound. However, the sound waves they create become intensified whenever they can reflect off of something. The open spaces inside our heads provide the perfect opportunity for such reflection. The resulting resonance provides amplification, complexity, and tone to our voices.

**To sing like never before**, making sound is easier than it sounds. Small adjustments to your breath, vocal folds, and resonance is all there is to it. Think about it—each time you sing, you're doing something that the silent universe cannot do. Who knows? The universe may even be jealous! In any case, never forget that infinity leans in to listen to you. The heavens themselves hope in hushed wonder to hear the joyful noises you create in the air.

---

  Discover your power supply by inhaling and exhaling with varying quantities and speeds of air.  Experience your vibratory source by touching your larynx and saying, "Ah." Feel the vibrations!  Explore your resonance by altering your lips, jaw, tongue, larynx, and soft palate as you sing.

## 22 Pitch — It Never Hz to Ask

Our Soprano paces anxiously in the wings. Awaiting her onstage is an awe-striking array of orchestral musicians. The audience applauds as the conductor takes a waist-bow and then gestures graciously to the oboe player. The oboist puffs an "*A Natural*." The entire orchestra instantaneously attempts to tune to this "Concert A" (aka "A440"). It's easy for *them*. Yet, if our soprano tries to sing this same A440, then her vocal folds are going to have to vibrate exactly 440 times per second!

How will she accomplish this seemingly impossible task?

## IT NEVER Hz TO ASK!

**PITCH** is the human ear's perception of musical notes depending on the frequency (vibrational speed) of sound waves. Frequency is measured in hertz (or Hz). We've learned that sound waves are vibrations that travel through the air. However, these vibrations can move slowly or quickly. If they travel slowly (fewer Hz), our ears perceive a lower musical note (or pitch). If they travel quickly (more Hz), our ears perceive a higher pitch.

*Musical pitch* is formed when these frequencies become organized in ways that are recognizable, predictable, or even beautiful to our ears. Every musical note has a corresponding frequency. The A440 to which the orchestra tunes travels at 440 sound waves per second (or 440 Hz). Every musical instrument that plays an A440 produces sounds waves that travel at that exact speed.

*Vocal pitch* is the frequency of the vocal folds' vibrations per second. For example, the tenor "high C" causes the vocal folds to vibrate at about 523 Hz. Meanwhile, some ultra-low notes that a bass might sing vibrate less than seventy times per second. Astonishingly, the soprano F6 vibrates at a soul-boggling 1,400 Hz!!!

So, we can certainly sympathize with our soprano's stress. Yet, there's still hope for her (and for us)! The vocal folds' superficial lamina propria are designed for fast vibrations. As long as she has a steady stream of breath, a healthy helping of resonance, and an energetic effort from the cricothyroid muscle, our soprano's vocal folds will be up to speed in no time!

**To sing like never before**, we don't need to suffer from pitch anxiety like our soprano. Was that high note flat? Don't take it personally. Your vocal folds just didn't vibrate fast enough. Are you going sharp? Then, take it easy! Your vocal folds can relax a bit. Keep calm and carry on pitch!

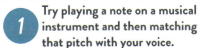 Try playing a note on a musical instrument and then matching that pitch with your voice.

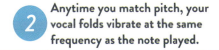 Anytime you match pitch, your vocal folds vibrate at the same frequency as the note played.

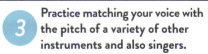 Practice matching your voice with the pitch of a variety of other instruments and also singers.

## 23 Timbre

HEAD SWAPPING

**EVER WISH THAT YOU COULD WALK IN SOMEONE ELSE'S SHOES FOR A DAY?**

**MAYBE YOU'D BORROW THE LITHE LEGS OF AN OLYMPIAN.**

**OR, YOU'D TEST-DRIVE THE DEXTEROUS DIGITS OF A CONCERT PIANIST.**

**OR, PERHAPS YOU'D STEAL THE STEALTHY SIGHT OF A SHARPSHOOTER.**

**BUT, IF IT'S THE TERRIFIC TIMBRE OF A SINGER YOU'RE TEMPTED TO TAKE — YOU'LL HAVE TO SWAP HEADS WITH THEM!**

**TIMBRE** is the distinctive resonance characteristics of a voice or musical instrument. Each person's natural vocal timbre is created primarily by the attributes of their head. Interestingly, if it were possible to switch heads with another person, you would probably end up sounding very much like them!

Heads come in all shapes and sizes. Each larynx, pharynx, nasal cavity, and mouth are built a bit differently. The qualities of these resonance spaces are unique to each individual, but they also change as we age. Ever wonder why babies make such a deafeningly high-pitched sound when they cry? It's those darling little resonance chambers!

Besides your head, there are other elements that can influence the uniqueness of your voice. Body structure, lung capacity, and vocal-fold size all factor into the power of your voice. Ethnicity, culture, and upbringing play a role in the tendencies your voice has. Musical influences, choices, and tastes help determine your vocal style. Training, experience, and practice result in your skillfulness.

Several other physical, mental, and emotional elements have the potential to alter the uniqueness of your voice. Yet, the most significant factor in determining your timbre is currently sitting atop your shoulders, reading a book about singing!

*"But what if I don't like my own unique timbre? I can't actually swap heads with another person—so what do I do?"* Good news! Timbre is adaptable! In fact, this is what vocal technique is all about. Just like the Olympian's legs, the concert pianist's fingers, and the sharpshooter's aim, the resonance of the singing voice must be developed! Mastery over the larynx, vocal folds, pharynx, jaw, lips, tongue, and soft palate is a lifelong pursuit that offers your voice infinite sonic possibilities.

**To sing like never before**, we don't need to swap heads with anyone. Instead, we need to embrace what we already have. There is no singer in the world who can change the unique head that they've been given. However, there is also no singer who cannot develop their unique characteristics into something extraordinary!

**1** Take a moment to celebrate the fact that your vocal timbre is truly one of a kind!

**2** Record yourself and listen back to observe the inherent qualities of your natural timbre.

**3** Start experimenting with the many ways (lips, tongue, larynx, etc.) that timbre can be altered.

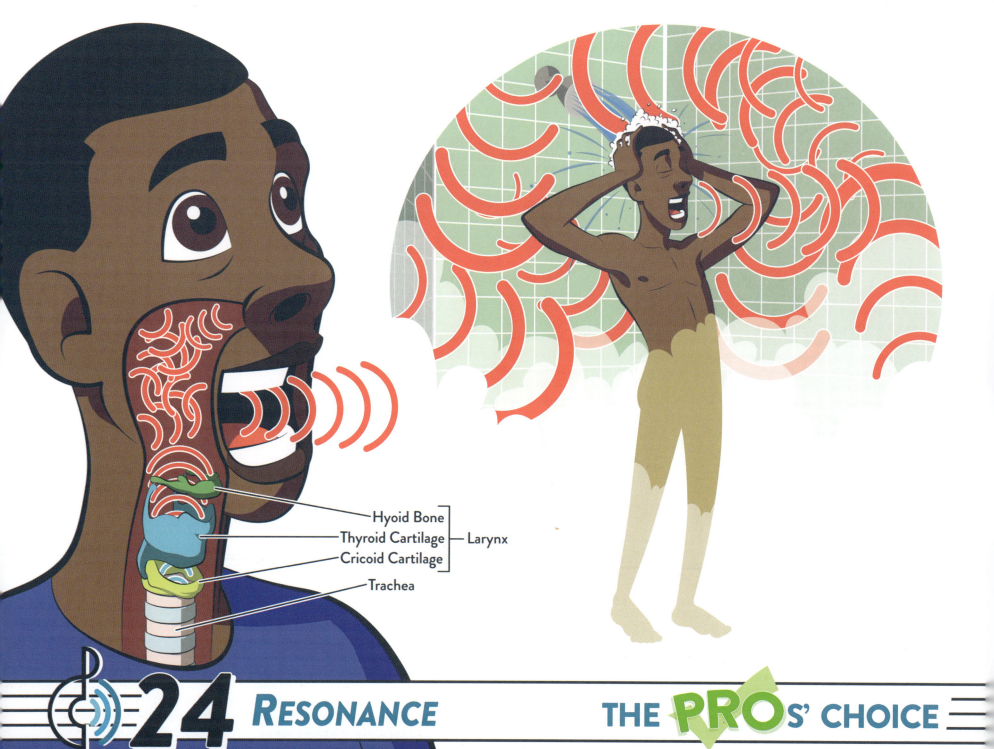

## 24 RESONANCE — THE PROS' CHOICE

- Hyoid Bone
- Thyroid Cartilage — Larynx
- Cricoid Cartilage
- Trachea

If you had the choice whether to give a free concert in the shower or in the park—which would you choose?
## LET'S WEIGH THE PROS AND THE CONS:

**PRO** If you sing in the shower, your voice will resound with acoustical awesomeness.

**CON** You will be naked.

**PRO** If you sing in the park, you will be clothed.

**CON** Your voice will sound a lot less lush.

**WHY? BECAUSE OF RESONANCE!**

**RESONANCE** is the intensification of sound waves within a space. In singing, this happens when sound waves reflect off of various chambers inside the head. The primary head spaces involved are the larynx, pharynx, mouth, and nasal cavity.

We've learned how our breath and our vocal folds work together to produce bursts of air that become sound waves. However, these waves get most of their unique and special characteristics from their interaction with the head's various chambers. Without our heads nearby, our vocal folds would still make a noise, but it wouldn't sound like much more than a blurred buzzing. How do we know?

Well, consider a guitar string. If you hold a detached string tightly with both of your hands and then pluck it, it will make a tiny tinny tone. String it onto a guitar, though, and suddenly an entirely new quality is created. Sound waves produced by the string's vibrations resonate inside the guitar's hollow body. Suddenly we hear a guitar instead of a meek metallic sound. What's even more fascinating, though, is that if you take the very same string and attach it to a banjo or other stringed instrument, it will adopt its resonance properties and sound like that instrument instead!

Another example is our lips. Try pressing your lips firmly together and blowing some air through them. You should be able to produce a buzzing vibration that amounts to only a small splatter of sound. However, place a trumpet in front of this buzz and it can blare with brassy brilliance. Place a trombone or tuba in front, and yet another unique noise results.

Hopefully, these examples resonate with you! In the upcoming sections, we'll see why the human voice has more resonance possibilities than any other musical instrument. We'll also examine the many ways that you can consciously change your own resonance by shaping the various chambers inside your head.

**To sing like never before**, let's get out of the shower before we are all washed up! Those dynamic ceramic tiles may give us a temporary boost, but their resonance is ultimately nothing more than a CON. Mastering your voice's resonance is the only way to become a PRO!

  **1** Sing in the shower and consider that similar reverberations are occurring inside your head.  **2** Experiment with any musical instrument that you have handy and ask: "How does it resonate?"  **3** If you dislike your current voice, remember that resonance can always be altered or improved.

## 25 VOWELS & FORMANTS

## EVER TRY IMITATING A MUSICAL INSTRUMENT WITH YOUR VOICE?

| What sound does a huge hollow upright bass make? Most people will say... | How about a brassy blaring trumpet? Maybe we could decide on... | A fluttery flute? Probably... | But wait a minute! |
|---|---|---|---|
|  | 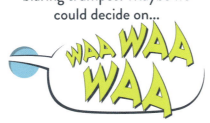 | TOO TOO TOO |  Clearly musical instruments can't sing like humans. So how can we agree that these instruments sound like these Vowels? |

**VOWELS** are sounds created by partially impeded air moving through the vocal tract. Adjustments to the jaw, tongue, and lips alter how air travels. Partially impeded airflow is needed for vowel sounds. However, when air is more fully impeded in various ways, consonants are created. For instance, when the tongue touches the hard palate like in a hiss, we get the consonant S. Or, when the lips block the mouth, we get consonants like B, P, or M. However, when the jaw, tongue, and lips do not significantly obstruct the airflow, the result is vowel sounds.

Vowels seem as easy as A, E, I, O, U. But, we still ask ourselves (sometimes), "Why?" Why does the human ear perceive vowels? Why do they differ from one another? And why do musical instruments often sound similar to vowels? The astonishing answer is that the voice is the only musical instrument that not only changes pitch, but also transforms itself into many different instruments (or resonance spectrums) as well!

As the vocal tract changes size and shape, various formants are created. *Formants* are resonance boosts that become amplified depending on the size and shape of the vocal tract. Vowels are determined by two primary resonance boosts known as Formant 1 (F1) and Formant 2 (F2). These two vowel formants give each vowel its own distinct sound quality.

For example, try speaking or singing a bright (trumpet-like) vowel like the AA vowel (as in "brass"). This vowel brings out a higher and brighter formant. Then, try a dark (bass-like) vowel like the UH vowel (as in "upright"). This vowel brings out a lower and darker formant. You should instantly notice how your voice resonates in a very different way, depending on the vowel shape you use.

**To sing like never before**, vowels must become more than just letters on a page. Instead, we must recognize them as resonance possibilities created by the vocal tract. If we can learn to manipulate these resonances, we maximize our acoustical capabilities. We may never be a bass, trumpet, or flute. But, thanks to vowels and formants, we can sound more like them than they'll ever sound like us!

1. Try imitating various musical instruments. Notice how your resonance varies dramatically.
2. Speak or sing several different vowels and observe how they alter your resonance.
3. In particular, compare bright vowels (like EE or AA) to dark vowels (like OH or UH).

## THE SINGING JURY HAS REACHED A VERDICT:

**THE MUSIC FAN SAYS:** Everyone knows that it's a crime to sing from the throat.

**THE CRITIC AGREES:** Ugh! Her tone was suspicious. Clearly she was singing ...FROM THE THROAT!

**EVEN GRANDMA ADMITS:** *SNIFF* I just wish she'd learned to not *SOB* SING FROM THE THROAT!

Objection! This singer is innocent! The court will be intrigued to learn that the voice's most important resonance cavity is actually the *throat itself*. So, in fact, the evidence shows that the more we "sing from the throat," the less guilty our voices are!

---

The **PHARYNX** is the open space of the throat that extends from the larynx to the nasal cavity. It is divided into three sections—the **LARYNGOPHARYNX**, the **OROPHARYNX**, and the **NASOPHARYNX**. Its anatomic function is to provide space for air, food, liquids, and bodily fluids to travel between the mouth, stomach, lungs, and nasal cavity.

The **LARYNGOPHARYNX** is the lowest section of the pharynx and is just what it sounds like: "the larynx pharynx." In other words, it's the part of the throat that relates to the larynx. Alterations to laryngopharyngeal space primarily involve movements of the larynx. Moving the larynx creates resonance shifts that are quite significant in altering or improving vocal tone.

When the larynx lowers, space in the laryngopharynx increases. This increased space enhances lower and darker resonances and generally accommodates louder volumes. When the larynx rises, space in the laryngopharynx decreases. This boosts higher and brighter resonances and generally accommodates softer volumes.

This is why, for example, opera singers generally sing with lower larynx positions than contemporary singers. Operatic singing is often darker in tone quality and requires the voice to be projected over an orchestra. Contemporary singing is usually brighter in tone quality and uses a microphone for its amplification.

Experiment with singing or speaking using different larynx positions. If you've never tried this, it's easier than you'd think. Simply imitate a deep-, hollow-, or "yawny-" sounding character to discover a lowered larynx. Imitate a bright-, piercing-, or whiny-sounding character to find a raised larynx. Moving between these different aesthetics will help you begin to understand the many resonance capabilities of your laryngopharynx.

**To sing like never before**, we won't plead ignorance to the laws of resonance. We will instead ask the court to uphold the larynx's inalienable right to change its position. If the laryngopharynx is granted full liberty in its pursuit of resonance, then good singing will abound! Throat open. Case closed.

---

 **SLNB QUICK TIPS**

**1** Speak or sing with a deep, hollow, or yawny character voice to discover a lowered larynx.

**2** Speak or sing with a bright, piercing, or whiny character voice to discover a raised larynx.

**3** Move between these extremes to master the resonance varieties of your laryngopharynx.

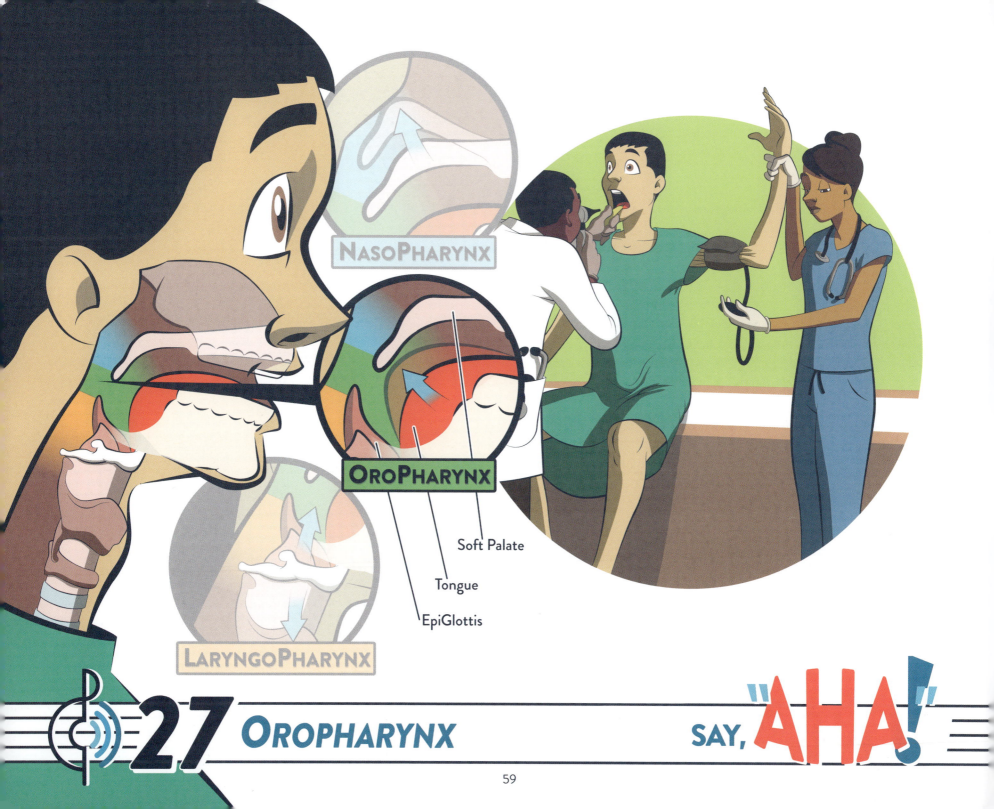

"SAY, AH!"

At your next visit to the doctor's office, that's probably the first thing you'll be asked. But, before they even ask, you can simply say,

IF YOU ARE PREPARED TO PERFORM YOUR OROPHARYNGEAL EXAMINATION, THEN I AM DELIGHTED TO OBLIGE YOU IN CREATING A RESONANCE CHAMBER THAT MAXIMIZES MY FIRST FORMANT FREQUENCIES.

Maybe the medical staff will be astonished with your knowledge. Or, maybe they will write "patient is difficult" on your chart. Either way, the doctor will need to get a good look at the back of your mouth. It's just a whole lot more fun to call it the "OROPHARYNX!"

---

The **OROPHARYNX** is the middle section of the pharynx located between the laryngopharynx and the nasopharynx. "Oro" means "mouth." So, the oropharynx can be thought of as the "mouth pharynx." The pharynx, as a whole, is the voice's primary source of resonance. However, resonance in the oropharynx operates very differently than it does in the laryngopharynx.

With the laryngopharynx, we saw that its size changes as the larynx moves. However, the size of the oropharynx is controlled by the constrictor muscles—which we don't usually want to tighten as a general rule in singing. The *constrictor muscles* wrap around the pharynx to help push food and liquids into the esophagus during swallowing. While this can play a part in brightening the voice, the vast majority of singers benefit from the image of an open throat. If you've never tried this, imagine that the back of your mouth is open, hollow, and relaxed while you sing. This should help you to not constrict your oropharynx!

Instead of being about size, resonance in the oropharynx is about various kinds of interference. Subtle adjustments made to the jaw and tongue impede air as it travels through the oropharynx. All vowels, consonants, and vocal sounds are made possible by different impediments and openings. Let's try a few!

Per the doctor's orders, we drop the jaw and tongue to say, "Ah!" The AH vowel allows the doctor to get the best look at the oropharynx. The mouth is impeded the least, while the tongue somewhat impedes the oropharynx. If the nurse brandishes a sharp needle, we say, "Eek!" The EE vowel has a more closed jaw and an elevated tongue position. In this case, the space in the oropharynx is quite open, while the tongue impedes the mouth.

As you sing, notice how drastically your resonance changes depending on the shapes you make with your jaw and tongue. Do you prefer more open vowels like AH or AW? Or, do you prefer more closed vowels like EE or OO? Neither way is wrong or right. But, knowing which shapes help your voice can be a clue to growing even further. If you find that a certain vowel consistently helps you, then try moving between that vowel and perhaps one that is more challenging for you (i.e. EE-AH). Or, you can even try alternating back and forth between the two (i.e. EE-AH-EE-AH). Over time, you will master a wide variety of vowels and shapes.

**To sing like never before**, the diagnosis is positive: All vocal sounds can resonate freely and clearly in the oropharynx. So, don't let your "EEKs" eke out your "AHs." Instead, explore all the ways that air can flow through your oropharynx. Say, "AHA!"

---

  Try singing an AH vowel. Then try singing an EE vowel. Does your voice have a preference?

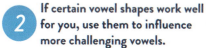 If certain vowel shapes work well for you, use them to influence more challenging vowels.

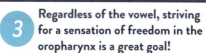 Regardless of the vowel, striving for a sensation of freedom in the oropharynx is a great goal!

    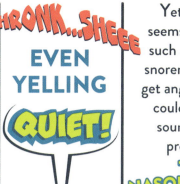

The **NASOPHARYNX** is the highest section of the pharynx, located above the oropharynx and laryngopharynx. It functions as a passageway between the nose and the throat. When air enters the nose, it travels through the nasal cavity, then the nasopharynx, and finally into the rest of the pharynx and the lungs. "Naso" means "nose." So, the nasopharynx can be thought of as the "nose pharynx." However, it shouldn't be confused with the nasal cavity itself. Just like the oropharynx is located behind the mouth, the nasopharynx is located behind the nasal cavity.

If you've never thought about your nasopharynx before, then try a snore! Snoring is the sound of the soft palate flapping around as air moves through the nasopharynx. Snoring is not the only sound made here, though. In fact, *all* vocal sounds involve the nasopharynx in some way. It's just a matter of determining the soft palate's position:

- With the soft palate fully raised, sounds resonate in the nasopharynx, but *not* the nasal cavity.

- With the soft palate somewhat lowered, sounds resonate in *both* the nasopharynx and the nasal cavity.

So, lowering the soft palate allows us to have nasal resonance in our voices. Conversely, raising the soft palate all the way up eliminates nasal resonance and causes our sound to only resonate in the pharynx and the mouth. We will explore nasal resonance vs. nasality more thoroughly in the upcoming sections.

Even though the nasopharynx is involved in every voiced sound, it becomes the most significant when we sing high notes. High notes are usually *felt* in the nasopharynx. Some of this is possibly due to the vocal folds stretching rearwards as they lengthen. Some is the result of the increased need for head resonance as pitches ascend. Either way, a good rule of thumb is: whenever your high notes are felt in that "snoring spot," they are resting in the right place.

**To sing like never before**, you've just got to have your beauty sleep. So, even though that loudmouth lying next to you is squandering your shut-eye, at least their snoring is good for something. You can sleep soundly, knowing where your high notes belong!

1. Discover the location of your nasopharynx by trying a snore or a snorting sound.

2. Try sliding from a low pitch to a high pitch. Feel and observe how the sensations change.

3. If you feel higher notes moving towards the nasopharynx, then this is a great sign!

# Hercules  Cyclops  Pegasus  Zeus  The Soft Palate

What do they have in common? They're all characters in some of mankind's greatest MYTHOLOGY. You don't even have to speak Greek. For if you've ever been told that "lifting the Soft Palate" will solve all your vocal problems, then you've already battled a legend of epic proportions!

The **SOFT PALATE** (velum) is a fleshy muscular divider that separates the nasal cavity from the pharynx. A fully-elevated soft palate blocks the nasal cavity during swallowing so that foods and liquids can enter the esophagus. If you've ever sprayed a beverage out your nose while laughing, then you recall when your soft palate literally *fell* in battle.

In vocal pedagogy antiquity, it was assumed that higher notes and proper resonance must be achieved by raising the soft palate. Unfortunately, this approach not only can make many higher notes more difficult, but it also can rob the voice of its full spectrum of resonance capabilities. So, how did the soft palate myth rise up?

In most singers, the larynx tends to raise too far as notes ascend, often resulting in a squeezed sound. Historically, this sound was often mislabeled as "nasal" because of its excessively bright (nasal) quality. Thus, singers were taught to raise the soft palate in an effort to combat this offensively bright tone, mistakenly called "nasality". The trouble is, this bright sound was never a product of the nasal cavity, but rather of a raised larynx and constricted pharynx.

In reality, a *very slight* lowering of the soft palate actually produces quite favorable outcomes for high notes and the voice as a whole. This is mostly due to the consistency and reliability of the resonance that it provides across all vocal registers. Nasal consonants (M, N, and NG) offer a practical illustration of this. Singing these consonants adds additional resonance, encourages vocal flexibility, helps blend vocal registers, assists with resonance continuity, and facilitates range development. These same benefits occur when small percentages of nasal resonance are added to any vowel (i.e. French nasal vowels or English words ending with a nasal consonant).

This doesn't mean that raising the soft palate is inherently negative. In fact, it raises naturally whenever we speak or sing any pure vowel sound. Thus, it's sensible to raise the soft palate anytime the purest vowel sounds are desired. On the other hand, a slightly lowered soft palate can be quite desirable whenever the benefits of nasal resonance supersede the need for total vowel purity. Regardless, obsessive focus on soft palate elevation often results in unwanted vocal habits like exaggerated lowered larynxes, retracted tongues, and unbalanced vocal registration. So, make sure your soft palate can go both ways!

For practice purposes, try vocalizing on a nasal consonant like M, N, or NG. As you do, notice the ease that this brings to your voice. From there, add a nasal consonant to the front and back of any vowel (i.e. "MAHM-MAHM" or "NEEN-NEEN"). You should notice that the vowel also takes on some of the ease and resonance of the nasal consonant. For a final product, make sure that your vowels have the ability to retain subtle amounts of this humming quality whenever desirable.

**To sing like never before**, become a vocal myth buster! Don't just lift your soft palate like Sisyphus pushing a boulder up a hill. Instead, develop heroic control over your soft palate's full range of motion. If you do, then vocal freedom will never be all Greek to you!

 **SLNB QUICK TIPS**

① Practice singing nasal consonants (M, N, and NG) to experience a lowered soft palate.

② Practice singing any pure vowel (like EE, OO, or AH) to experience a raised soft palate.

③ Practice nasalized vowels (like MAHM or NEEN) to experience an "in between" soft palate.

Have you ever been accused of sounding too "nasal"? If so, it seems like it wouldn't take a Sherlock Holmes to figure out where this "Nasality" comes from. But, in fact, one cannot just follow their nose! It really does take a singing sleuth to solve this particularly perplexing puzzle. The usual suspects have already been ruled out—the soft palate, the nasal cavity, and even the nose itself! So, we must decipher who's responsible for these unwanted "nasally" sounds.

**NASALITY** is a term most commonly used to describe undesirably bright qualities in a voice. Meanwhile, *nasal resonance* is resonance that involves some degree of nasal airflow via a slightly lowered soft palate.

While it's certainly possible to use too much nasal resonance, the most common misuse of the term "nasality" doesn't necessarily involve the nasal cavity at all. Very bright tone can occur regardless of whether the soft palate is raised or lowered. Moreover, nasal resonance can also be used when singing with a deep, rich, and full vocal tone.

Gadzooks! It seems that "nasality" has been used inappropriately all along! With a misnomer like "nasality" floating about, it's easy to see why the nasal cavity, nose, and soft palate have long been under such scrutinous suspicion. Yet, as it turns out, nasal resonance doesn't actually cause extreme brightness at all. Instead, we must turn our attention to twang.

*Twang* is a vocal tone quality that amplifies higher and brighter resonances (formants). Twang is produced by narrowing the supraglottic area (the place right above your vocal folds). This can be done by pushing the epiglottis back, lifting the larynx, or constricting the walls of the pharynx— or a combination of any of the three.

If you'd like to experience twang, perhaps the best way is by imitating a character voice. Some classic speech examples include a crying baby, an irritating buzzer, a quacking duck, or a nagging mosquito. Other classic singing examples include stereotypical country music singers, excessively brassy musical theatre singers, or very high rock or gospel wailers. In all of these examples, there is a boost in the higher frequencies (brighter resonances) of the voice.

Remember that smaller resonance chambers intensify higher frequencies and larger spaces intensify lower frequencies. Thus, when the space above the vocal folds is narrowed, it helps to boost brighter resonances. While it's possible for twang to be created somewhat independently from larynx position, brighter resonances are almost always accompanied by a lifted larynx. In both the cases of twang and of higher larynx positions, sound waves resonate in smaller chambers that result in brighter resonances.

So, ultimately these bright resonances have nothing to do with the nasal cavity. And this gives us our answer: "nasality" (when used as a misnomer) is the fault of smaller larynx and pharynx spaces—but *not* of the nasal cavity! Brilliant deduction, Sherlock!

**To sing like never before**, we must solve one of singing's greatest mysteries once and for all. Worried about sounding too nasal? Don't automatically blame your nasal resonance! Instead, begin practicing a more relaxed, deep, and open larynx and throat. On the other hand, if you are seeking a bright, brilliant, and brassy resonance, then you might as well recruit the services of twang. It's elementary, my dear singers!

 **1** Be certain that you don't automatically mislabel offensively bright vocal qualities as nasality. **2** Discover twang by imitating a crying baby, an irritating buzzer, or a nagging mosquito. **3** Challenge yourself to create twang with and without moving sound into the nasal cavity.

# CHAPTER 4
## POSTURE & ALIGNMENT

# 31 Feet

# A DOUBLE THREAT

Other less terpsichoreally-talented troubadours are told that they've got "TWO LEFT FEET."

# THAT'S TRULY TROUBLESOME!

Why? First of all, nothing ever seems to go well—life never starts off on the RIGHT FOOT! Plus, Left Feet are expensive—you always have to buy two pairs of shoes and trash the right sides of each pair. Finally, you can never win at Twister—you have to forfeit every time someone calls out "Right Foot—Green." Thankfully, your singing voice still has a leg to stand on!

---

The **FEET** are a foundational factor for posture, alignment, and balance in singing. Good posture isn't limited just to the spine. In fact, spinal alignment can be impacted by the feet's position anytime we stand. Although there are certainly times when we're sitting, walking, or dancing, the majority of singing takes place while standing. This is why it's helpful to get our feet right in terms of their position and weight distribution.

Ideally, we want to imagine the feet as a tripod with three distinct points:

① The first point is located at the ball of the foot.

② The second point is located just below the pinky toe.

③ The third point is located at the heel.

In an ideal weight distribution, two-thirds of the weight should be distributed toward the front of the feet, while one-third should be distributed toward the back.

It's pretty obvious why bringing the weight too far toward the front is problematic. This would cause us to topple forwards. Yet, a much more common problem occurs whenever our weight plummets backwards into the heels. A postural chain reaction often takes place. The knees tend to fall backwards and lock. The pelvis then torques too far forward. The combination of these events begins to affect our breathing system, not allowing it to function optimally. We also appear lazy, logy, and lethargic.

In short, allowing the weight to sink back into our heels can compromise our breathing, alignment, mobility, and appearance. So, when standing to sing, make sure to take some time to find your balance. Begin by rocking back and forth between the front and back of your feet until you find equilibrium. The rest of your posture and alignment will fall into place much more easily from there.

**To sing like never before**, we can't dance around the importance of the feet. While some of us may have left feet with a 2-0 advantage, we can still have our weight distributed evenly. After all, good posture and alignment should never be an impossible feat!

---

  Rock back and forth on your feet until you find a two-thirds to one-third equilibrium.  Notice how this creates an ideal foundation for the rest of your posture and alignment.  As you sing, be mindful to not let your weight start falling back in your heels.

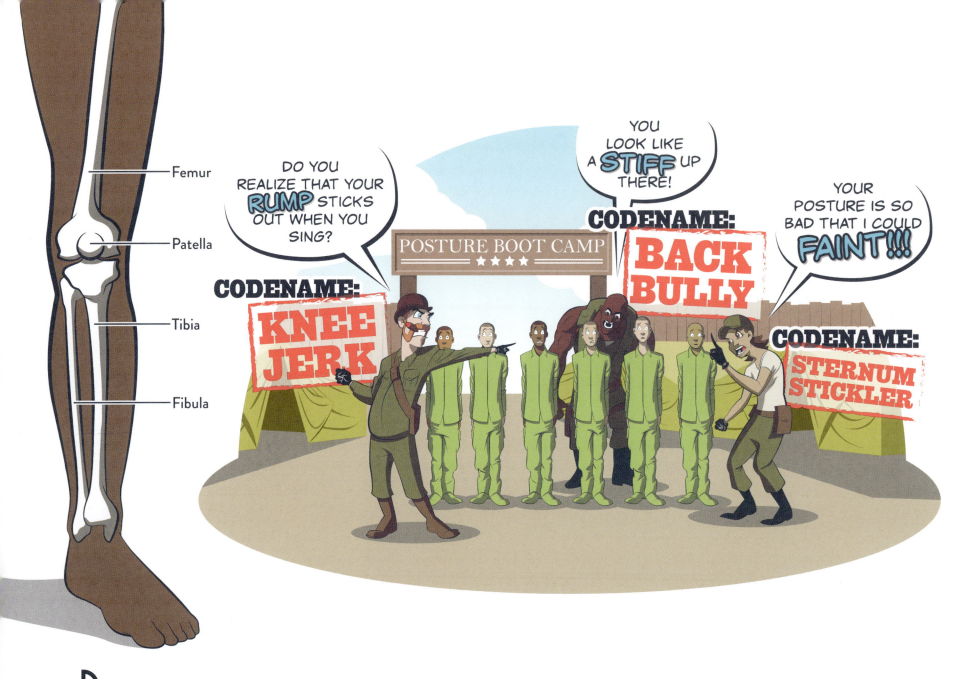

| Posture doesn't need  POLICING it needs PERCEPTIVENESS | Alignment doesn't need  ANTAGONISM it needs ATTENTION | Let's not have a  |

The **KNEES** are the largest joint in the human body. Just like the hyoid bone, the knees possess great range of motion. This allows them to bend and move in a wide variety of ways. Nevertheless, it's a common habit for singers to lock their knees, or hold them in a state of extension. This can be the result of poor posture, physical rigidity, or even performance anxiety. Regardless of the cause, it's easy to see why postural problems increase exponentially when the body's largest joint becomes locked.

## ALIGNMENT
Alignment is the primary problem. Locking the knees usually causes the pelvis to tilt forward. In turn, this can impact the breathing system by creating stress and tension in the lumbar spine and lower rib cage.

## MOBILITY
Mobility is a secondary concern. Singers need to be free to move around while performing. If the knees are extended backwards, then movement becomes quite difficult. This often results in a stiff onstage appearance.

## FAINTING
Fainting is a rare, but noteworthy possibility. Occasionally very nervous singers will freeze up during a performance and clench their knees tightly for long durations. Doing this in a severe fashion can cut off blood circulation and lead to syncope (passing out) in extreme cases. While this isn't something to fear, it is certainly an additional incentive for remaining aware of the knees.

Thankfully, of all postural considerations, the knees are perhaps the easiest to address. The solution is usually as simple as maintaining a slight bend in the knees while singing. Knee pedaling (slight alternating bends) or pliés (full knee bends) are also beneficial during practice sessions.

Both knee pedaling and pliés utilize movement to ensure physical freedom. They also simultaneously release tension in the hips and lower back. Try these gestures and you will quickly notice high notes, difficult phrases, and challenging vocal tasks becoming easier to execute from a physical standpoint.

**To sing like never before**, don't let the posture police jerk you around. Good posture should never look postured. Instead, the pliable must become the reliable. The lithe must become the blithe. The bendable must become the dependable. At ease, knees!

 For optimal posture and alignment, make sure to maintain a very slight bend in the knees.

 Try knee pedaling and pliés during high notes, difficult phrases, or challenging vocal tasks.

 Remember that good posture never involves holding the body in a stiff or rigid fashion.

Because any tension in the vicinity of the Elvis Pelvis simply must be "all SHOOK UP." After all, it doesn't take a KING to understand that **physical freedom** and **vocal freedom** are literally joined at the HIPS!

The **HIPS** play a significant role in both vocal technique and performance. For technique purposes, the hips serve as a kind of hub for several breathing muscles. The rectus abdominis, transverse abdominis, obliques, and quadratus lumborum are all exhalation muscles that attach to the hips and pelvis.

Rigidity in the hips encourages tension in these muscles. On the other hand, freedom in the hips allows for their suppleness, control, and ease. As we've learned, breath support requires us to not engage our exhalation muscles too much or too fast as we sing. So, it makes perfect sense that singers with freer hips will usually have better breath support and control!

In performance, hip rigidity prevents performers from appearing natural or at home on stage. In contrast, hip freedom is generally associated with spontaneity, sexuality, and confidence. This certainly is not to suggest that Elvis-styled pelvic gyrations are necessary or appropriate for most performances! However, maintaining some mobility in the hips can create a noticeable difference in your appearance, psyche, and stage presence.

Two primary strategies can help maximize freedom in your hips. The first strategy is stretching. Hip stretches such as lunges, pigeon pose, and butterfly pose are all very effective for releasing tension in the hips. These kinds of stretches can be performed before or even during a vocal workout.

The second strategy is movement. You don't have to be Elvis Presley to move your hips while you practice. In fact, doing so has surprising results. Moving the pelvis front to back, side to side, or in a circular motion while vocalizing keeps the hips and their surrounding muscles supple and pliant. Give it a try! It may feel a bit unusual to you at first. Eventually though, your voice "can't help falling in love" with the increased physical freedom and the deeper connection to the breath.

**To sing like never before**, it's now or never! Time to shake it till you make it! If your hips will start letting go, then your voice will say: "A thank ya. Thank ya very much."

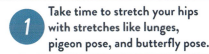
1. Take time to stretch your hips with stretches like lunges, pigeon pose, and butterfly pose.

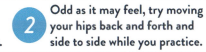
2. Odd as it may feel, try moving your hips back and forth and side to side while you practice.

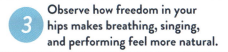
3. Observe how freedom in your hips makes breathing, singing, and performing feel more natural.

The **LOWER BACK** is a pivotal region for posture and alignment. Yet, many singers habitually round and curve the lower back too far while standing to sing. This becomes particularly pronounced when performing in high-heeled shoes or on raked stages (sloped stages).

Lower back tension is often caused by improper weight distribution in the feet, locking of the knees, and misalignment of the hips. These issues frequently occur in singers' everyday stances. However, high heels and raked stages greatly exacerbate the problem because of the additional compensation they require.

It's important to remember that a natural curvature exists in the lumbar spine. Thus, fully straightening this curvature should never be a goal. However, when the lower back is excessively rounded, tightened, or torqued, the rib cage becomes compromised. Since the rib cage is critical for breathing, almost all lower back tension and misalignment negatively impacts the breathing system. This is why singers often find lower back breathing to be a helpful concept.

*Lower back breathing* is the expansion of the lumbar region during inhalation. This area is not nearly as expandable as the abdomen or rib cage. Nevertheless, some expansion can be felt. Give it a try! Place a hand on your lower back and allow it to expand as you inhale. You'll immediately notice that lower back breathing complements the efficiency of both your intercostal and abdominal breathing systems. It will also help you to reduce the tendency to use clavicular breathing or take in too much air.

Singers who suffer from recurring lower back tension might also need to spend time stretching before practices and performances. Ideal stretches include folding forward at the hips, rounding the spine (cat/cow pose), and bringing the knees toward the chest (child's pose). All of these movements help to relieve tension and balance out any exaggerated curvature in the lower back.

**To sing like never before**, high heels don't have to be your Achilles' heel. Raked stages don't have to rake your posture over the coals. Just make sure that before you go out there, you're confident that lower back tension won't crash the party!

**1** Use lower back breathing to free up tension in this area as well as for better breath efficiency.

**2** Perform stretches like forward folds, cat/cow pose, and child's pose to open the lower back.

**3** Avoid trying to fully straighten the lower back, but instead allow for its natural curvature.

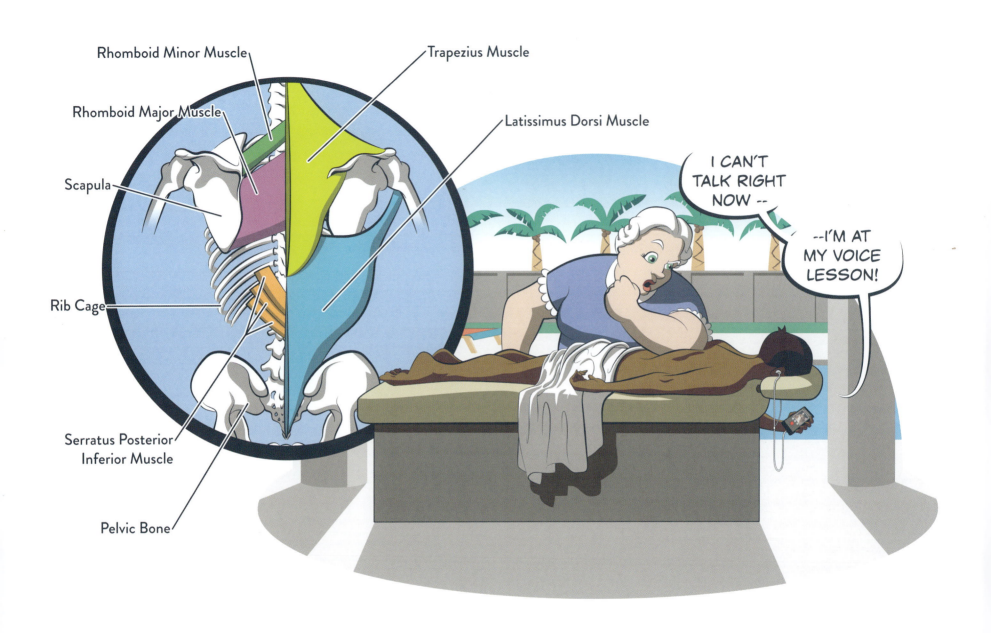

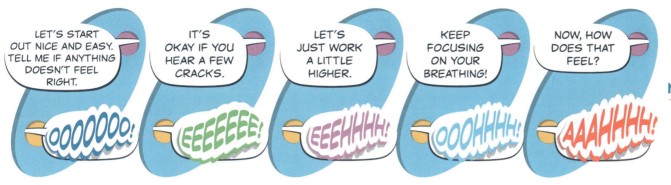

The **UPPER BACK** is a common area for muscle tension. In life, this can be uncomfortable or even painful. Of course, this is why massages often focus on relieving tight or sore muscles in this area. In singing, the same kind of tension in the upper back can also create several limitations and difficulties.

Singers are frequently told to stand up straight. This is generally good and well-intentioned advice. However, there's a big difference between posture and becoming postured. In an effort to have good posture, many singers exaggerate by placing unwanted tension in the upper back and narrowing the distance between the *scapulae* (shoulder blades).

While exaggerating may give the *appearance* of good posture, it actually creates other problems—particularly for the rib cage. You probably recall that intercostal breathing (rib breathing) is one of our most advantageous breathing types. Thus, the rib cage must be free to move during singing. However, the rib cage's mobility is restricted when the upper back carries tension. This makes intercostal breathing much more difficult to execute. As a result, singers often have to compensate by reverting to clavicular breathing.

So, can we relieve upper back tension without a trip to the massage parlor? Absolutely! The most effective strategy is to move your arms into the ballet fifth position. If you're not familiar with this, it's the equivalent of pretending to hug a giant tree trunk. Give it a try! Once you're in this position, take several full breaths. With each inhale, feel the upper back, the rib cage, and the area between the scapulae expand more and more. It should feel quite energizing when you do this. After you've breathed open your upper back, drop your arms. The position you're left with is a wonderful middle ground—straight and upright, but without exaggerating to the point of upper back tension. From this balanced position, try some singing. You should feel an immediate sense of ease to your alignment and breath.

**To sing like never before**, you don't need fancy oils, soothing ocean sounds, or a hot towel. But, one way or another, you do need some freedom in the upper back. So, open up your shoulder blades and breathe.

 Observe whether any upper back tension is affecting your ability to breathe or move freely.

 Take several breaths in the ballet fifth position to open up the upper back and rib cage.

 The space between your scapulae should always feel wide and open as you breathe and sing.

Many moons ago, there lived  a Sloth, a Hero, and a Dragon. All of them dreamed of wooing the lovely Singing Maiden and winning her hand. Yet, woefully—none of them knew how to sing. Lacking knowledge of vocal technique, all three were deeply perplexed and carried the weight of the world on their Shoulders.

The **SHOULDERS** can impact the breathing system, depending on their alignment and movement. Thus, the shoulders are not just a vexation for our three suitors. They can be a problem for any singer. So, let's learn from our fable.

## SLOTH SHOULDERS

The sloth was pure of heart, but lacked confidence. He moped around with his shoulders slumping down and forwards. This collapsed his rib cage and put pressure on his abdomen. When the sloth sang for the maiden, he sounded dull and unenergized. "Too weak. Too meek," said she.

## HERO SHOULDERS

The hero was noble and valiant, but arrogant too. He strutted about the vocal kingdom with his shoulders back and chest out. Lamentably, this caused tension between his scapulae and restricted movement in his rib cage. When the hero sang for the maiden, he sounded rigid and squeezed. "Too tight. Not right," said she.

## DRAGON SHOULDERS

The dragon was fiery and passionate, but was wont for grace. When he breathed in, his shoulders and mighty wings lifted up. Breathing out, they dropped violently and forcefully. This caused intense clavicular breathing and a "pushed" sounding voice. When the dragon sang for the maiden, he charred her climbable chestnut locks! "Too strong! All wrong!" shrieked she.

## SINGER SHOULDERS

The singing maiden was the finest singer in all the vocal kingdom. Her mellifluous tone enraptured the hearts of both man and beast. Such exquisiteness was by virtue of her shoulders remaining perfectly aligned at all times. Not too far forward as to appear lazy and slothful. Not too far back as to appear haughty and heroic. And certainly not moving up and down in a volcanic panic! When she sang, the sloth, hero, and dragon recognized their errors forthwith. "So easy. I'm queasy," wept all three.

What's the moral of our fable? *Shoulder position can influence our vocal destiny.* So, start by moving your shoulders back and forth. Find their ideal balance right in the middle. Next, lift your shoulders up and drop them down fast. This establishes a relaxed, yet confident position. From there, keep your shoulders calm, stable, and poised as you sing. As you practice this noble posture, notice how much easier your breathing feels. Plus, you're already starting to look like royalty!

**To sing like never before**, we must appreciate the moral of our fable. It was needless for the sloth, hero, and dragon to place such burdens on their shoulders in order to sing. Alas, their match was not maiden heaven!

 Move your shoulders from slouched to thrust back. The ideal is right between these extremes.

 Lift your shoulders and then drop them down fast. This also helps achieve your ideal balance.

 Well-aligned shoulders improve technique, but also convey confidence and poise on stage.

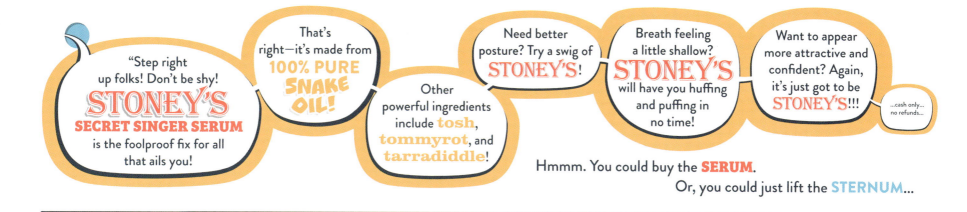

Hmmm. You could buy the **SERUM**.
Or, you could just lift the **STERNUM**...

The **STERNUM** is a flat bone that runs from the top of the clavicle to the middle of the chest. The sternum has a considerable influence on posture and breathing. In fact, lifting the sternum is perhaps the single most transformative postural adjustment you can make as a singer. Give it a try! Lift your sternum subtly without adding tension in your upper back or shoulder blades. Feel the difference? Just this one simple change creates results that can seem too good to be true!

## BREATHING

Lifting the sternum improves breath support by creating space in both the rib cage and the abdomen. The sternum is actually a *part* of the rib cage. So, whenever the sternum is lifted, the ribs have an easier time staying lifted. The sternum also connects to the abdominal muscles. Thus, an elevated sternum allows rectus abdominis to be expansive and free from tension. As a result, both the intercostal and abdominal muscles gain a significant advantage with the sternum raised.

## POSTURE

The sternum also influences the head, neck, and larynx. As the sternum collapses, the back of the neck shortens and tightens. This is a common symptom of innumerable hours spent slumping in front of phones, computer screens, and steering wheels. Head and neck misalignment directly contribute to tension in the larynx. Thankfully, the sternum can once again remedy this. Just by lifting the sternum, the neck lengthens and the head moves back into alignment instantly—almost as if by magic!

## AESTHETICS

Lastly, lifting the sternum flat-out looks good! An elevated sternum gives the appearance of confidence and self-assurance. Conversely, a collapsed sternum tends to convey shyness, sadness, or insecurity. Since performers need to exude confidence, lifting the sternum is an ideal first choice!

**To sing like never before**, there's no need for snake oil serums or hocus pocus potions. Lifting the sternum is a much better way to improve posture, breathing, and appearance. It's so effective that it's liable to put old Stoney out of the snake oil business!

---

  Lift your sternum and take a few breaths. Notice increased efficiency in both the ribs and abs. 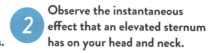 Observe the instantaneous effect that an elevated sternum has on your head and neck.  Consider lifting your sternum not just for singing, but for improving posture in everyday life.

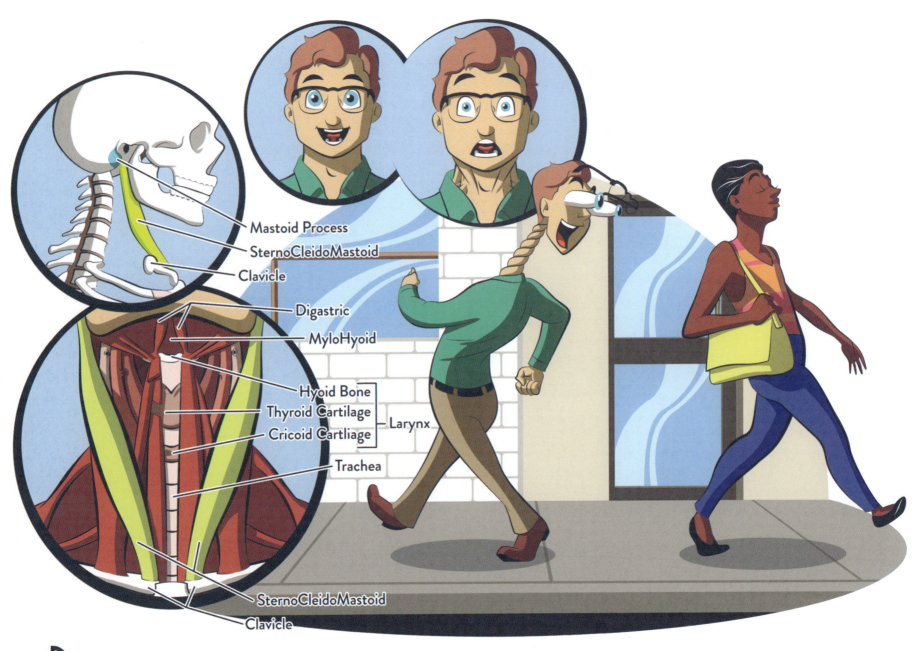

# 38 THE STERNOCLEIDOMASTOID — A REAL HEAD-TURNER

The **STERNOCLEIDOMASTOIDS** (SCMs) are neck muscles used primarily for turning the head. The top of the SCMs attach to the mastoid process, which is located at the back of the head behind the ears. The second attachment point is the top of the clavicle.

The SCMs are the largest neck muscles, and play a key role in neck and head alignment. They turn the head from side to side (chin to shoulder), and also obliquely (ear to shoulder). They can also tense and flex the neck, assisting with jutting the head forward. Lastly, the SCMs sometimes act as secondary breathing muscles by helping raise the clavicle during inhalation. To feel your SCMs, place a hand gently on the front of your neck and try any of these movements.

In singing, it can be challenging to differentiate between our intrinsic larynx muscles and our extrinsic larynx muscles (like the SCMs). *Intrinsic larynx muscles* are muscles located inside the larynx. Typically, these tiny muscles are the most difficult yet most important to isolate and control.

*Extrinsic larynx muscles* are muscles located outside the larynx. These include muscles of the neck, jaw, and tongue. Extrinsic larynx muscles are larger, stronger, and thus more intuitive for many singers to use. Unfortunately, the result is often some degree of strain and tension.

The SCMs are perhaps the most notorious of the extrinsic larynx muscles. Their ability to tense the neck, jut the head forward, and put pressure on the larynx make them among the most common contributors to vocal strain. Luckily, sternocleidomastoid tension is also the easiest vocal habit to see. You will notice a very obvious sort of V-shape at the front of your neck anytime your SCMs become involved.

This extrinsic visibility makes any SCM issues quite simple to solve—especially when compared to the subtleties of the intrinsic larynx muscles. In fact, significant progress can be made toward reducing your vocal tension simply by bringing awareness to the SCMs during practice sessions. By using a mirror, you will instantly notice if your SCMs are interfering. From here, it should be quite easy to let go of this muscle tension just by inviting a feeling of expansion to the front of your neck. You'll also want to make sure that your head is not jutting forward as you sing. If this is still not enough, then you can place a few fingers gently into the SCMs to help them to calm down.

**To sing like never before**, we need to look the other way when it comes to the sternocleidomastoids. While they may help us spot the most stunning person in the room, they also limit our voices. So, don't strain your SCMs every time a hunk, hottie, or high note approaches. Seek first their Intrinsic qualities!

 With a hand placed gently on your neck, turn your head side to side to locate your SCMs.

 Observe your SCMs in the mirror while singing to become aware of any tension they may hold.

 If you see a V-shape while singing, imagine widening your neck to help free your SCMs.

It's as easy as *1-2-3*! With the Tension Treatment Trifecta, you can deliberately relieve tension from most muscles. Especially those that are a real pain in the NECK...

The **NECK** is a critical area for singing because it houses both the larynx and the vocal folds. We've just explored the neck's largest muscles (*sternocleidomastoids*). However, the neck also contains both larynx-lowering muscles (*sternothyroid, sternohyoid,* and *omohyoid*) *and* larynx-raising muscles (*thyrohyoid, stylohyoid, geniohyoid, mylohyoid,* and *digastric*). Thus, laryngeal freedom requires the neck to be absent of tension. Enter the Tension Treatment Trifecta...

###  STRETCHING

Neck stretches are simple, but produce very beneficial results. Try some! Begin with a neutral head position. Then, move your chin to the twelve standard clock positions. *(Three o'clock is to the right, six o'clock is straight down, etc.)* Move to each position one by one, or roll through them. (Be sure to not hang your head back as you do these, as this can be unsafe.) Pause in each position and take a few breaths. Try stretching your jaw and tongue in each position as well. This should all be performed mindfully and should never cause any pain. In addition to eliminating tension, neck stretches make a great physical warmup prior to singing.

###  MOVING

Keeping the head in motion while singing is another method for combating tension. A subtle head bobble or small figure-eight can be enough to ensure that neck muscles don't seize up. While some artists iconically incorporate head movements like these into their actual performances, all singers can benefit from this during practice.

###  HOLDING

Physically holding extrinsic muscles is the most direct and effective strategy for eliminating tension. This can be done by pressing a few fingers gently yet purposefully into overactive muscles. It's easy to identify whether unwanted muscles are tightening or straining by keeping a mirror nearby during practice sessions.

Singers are sometimes hesitant about touching neck muscles due to their proximity to the larynx. In reality though, neck muscles are no different than any other muscle and are safe to touch. Physical touch is often the missing solution for overcoming pesky muscle habits that in many cases have persisted for years.

**To sing like never before**, muscle tension must be vanquished via stretching, moving, and holding—aka the Tension Treatment Trifecta. The TTT is as easy as ABC for giving your neck a little TLC!

 Try some neck stretches in the various clock positions as a warmup or to free up tension.

 Move your head in small figure-eight circles or side to side while practicing.

 Press gently into neck muscles as a safe and effective strategy for combating tension.

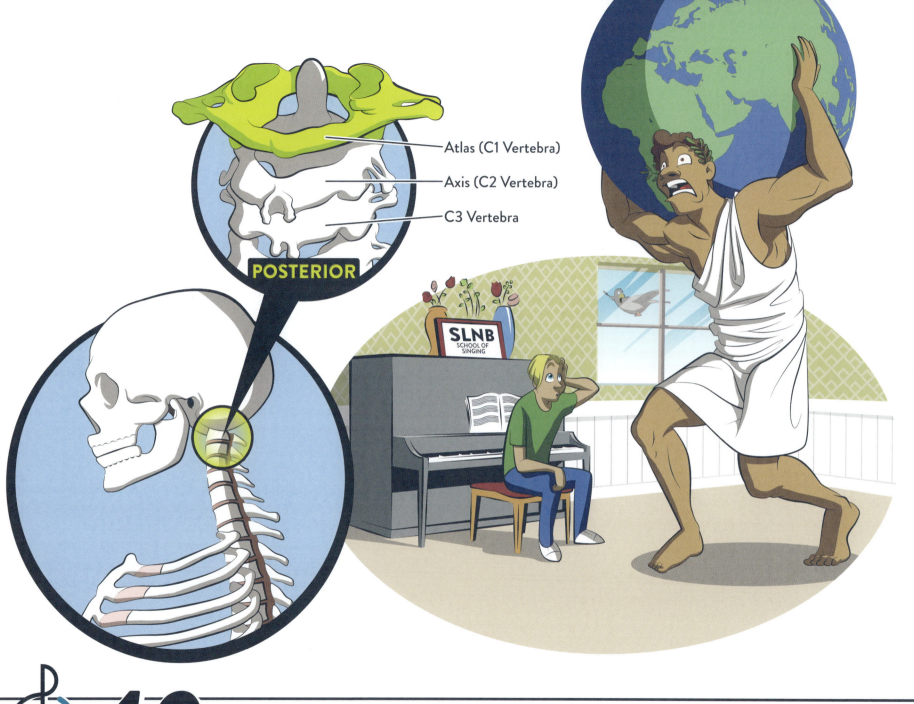

## FEEL LIKE YOU'RE "IN OVER YOUR HEAD" SOMETIMES?

Well, tell that to Atlas.

His punishment is to bear the heavens on his shoulders for all eternity! All that "heaven carrying" business will certainly not go over well with his voice teacher. Vocal technique is hard enough. But, it's downright impossible when your Head is in the clouds!

The **HEAD** is our primary source of vocal resonance. So, it's especially important that it not be compromised by postural problems. Many people don't realize that the spine doesn't stop at the shoulders and neck. Rather, it goes all the way up to the head!

The *atlas* (C1 vertebra) is the topmost vertebra of the spine. The head, neck, and spine all converge at the atlas to coordinate the head's position and regulate its ability to move. Most head alignment issues can be identified and corrected at the atlas.

One common issue is jutting the head outward. This habit compromises the atlas by bringing it too far forward. Head jutting is especially prevalent when singers reach for higher notes. This encourages unwanted laryngeal elevation as well as participation from extrinsic muscles of the neck, jaw, and tongue. Be mindful of keeping your head above your shoulders and not awkwardly extending it forward—especially as notes get higher.

Another frequent habit is the tendency to look up for higher notes and down for lower notes. This doesn't necessarily compromise the atlas, but it does reinforce certain laryngeal habits. As pitches ascend, the larynx tends to lift. As pitches descend, the larynx tends to lower. Some of this movement is natural and unavoidable. However, if excessive larynx movement is a problem for you, then it is advantageous to minimize the tendency as much as possible. To help with this, keep your head as stable as you can with respect to pitch.

A third issue happens when singers overcompensate for the first two issues. In an effort to reduce head movement and forward thrusting, it can be tempting to go to extremes. Singers sometimes pull the head backwards and upwards to essentially straighten out the neck. However, just like the lower back, the neck should have a natural curvature. This curvature must be honored and maintained for the atlas to remain free from tension and manipulation. So, make sure you don't try to straighten your neck for good posture. If your head and neck feel out of alignment, try lying on a firm surface with a small book beneath your head. This can help to reset your alignment in the head and neck.

**To sing like never before**, the head should never feel like the weight of the heavens. Instead, it should always move freely as it sits atop the atlas—never forced backwards, forwards, up, or down. So, while it's important to have a good head on your shoulders, it's even more important how you keep it there!

  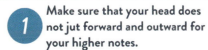 Make sure that your head does not jut forward and outward for your higher notes.  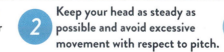 Keep your head as steady as possible and avoid excessive movement with respect to pitch.  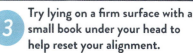 Try lying on a firm surface with a small book under your head to help reset your alignment.

# CHAPTER 5
## THE TONGUE, JAW, & MOUTH

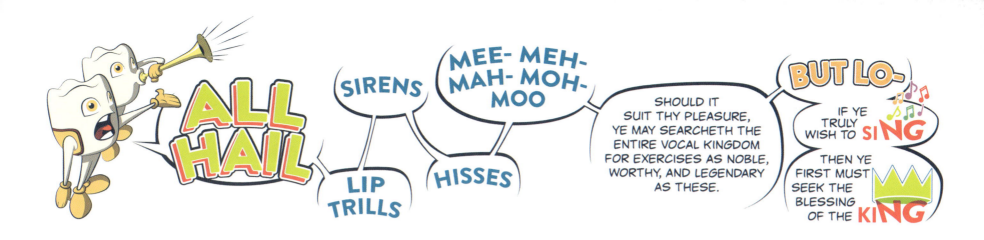

The **NG TONGUE POSITION** is the shape formed by the tongue when it produces the nasal consonant NG. *Nasal consonants* are phonemes that block air from exiting the mouth, causing sound to resonate dominantly in the pharynx and nasal cavity. M does this by bringing the lips together. N does this by bringing the tongue tip to the hard palate. In the case of NG, the *base* of the tongue elevates (via the palatoglossus muscle) to meet the soft palate. So, what makes NG the reigning KiNG of all vocal exercises?

### FREEDOM

First, the NG tongue position promotes the freedom of *both* the jaw and the tongue. To discover the ideal NG tongue position, begin by letting your mouth open and your jaw relax downwards and backwards. The tip of your tongue should rest at the gumline of the bottom teeth. If your tongue is fully relaxed, the base should elevate in the back and then slope downward toward the teeth. You'll quickly notice that the NG tongue position feels like the epitome of a relaxed jaw and tongue.

### RESONANCE AND FLEXIBILITY

Next, vocalizing on pure NG ensures that all notes establish their maximum head and nasal resonance. Practice singing a pure NG on some scales or a song. With air unable to escape the mouth, resonance becomes 100 percent focused in the pharynx, nasopharynx, and nasal cavity. This dramatically improves the voice's flexibility because all pitches resonate in the same way. In other words, as you sing across your range, NG helps you gain consistency and ease by offering you a reliable and stable resonance.

### VOWEL PLACEMENT

Lastly, the NG tongue position can assist all vowel sounds in achieving nasal resonance. To do this, NG can be easily opened into any vowel. For example, try *NG-AH* or *NG-OH*. Another option is to alternate between a vowel and the NG several times. For example, try *NG-EE-NG-EE*. With a little practice, nasal resonance can be added to any vowel that has been graced by NG's presence.

**To sing like never before**, ye must NG like never before! With so many regal provisions—freedom of jaw and tongue, abundance of vocal flexibility, and magnificence of resonance—we must humbly proclaim: Long live the KiNG!

---

**SLNB QUICK TIPS**

1. Establish an NG consonant by speaking or singing the word "king" and lingering on the NG.
2. Practice exercises or songs on NG to improve resonance, flexibility, and jaw/tongue freedom.
3. Alternate NG with vowels (i.e. NG-AH-NG-AH) to discover nasal resonance on all vowels.

Tongue (Glossus)
PalatoGlossus
GenioGlossus
StyloGlossus
HyoGlossus
Hyoid Bone
Thyroid Cartilage

## 42 TONGUE RETRACTION — SINGING'S SPELUNKER

**TONGUE RETRACTION** occurs when the tongue leaves its natural resting position and retreats backwards into the pharynx. The styloglossus muscle is responsible for this action as the tongue (glossus) is brought toward the styloid process (stylo-). In other words, the tongue is pulled into the throat. Additionally, the hyoglossus muscle often plunges the tongue's base downward toward the larynx.

To experience tongue retraction, slowly say the word "spelunker." Notice how the tongue travels further and further back into the "cave" of the pharynx as you approach the "er" sound. While tongue retraction happens naturally in speech during certain approximant consonants (like L and R), it can create several problems in singing...

### BULLYING THE LARYNX

Perhaps the worst problem created by tongue retraction is the forceful lowering of the larynx. The tongue's base is only millimeters from the larynx. Thus, exaggerated backward and downward tongue movement instantly bullies the larynx into a lowered position and compromises its free range of motion. If you need a lower larynx for your vocal style, make sure that your tongue isn't shoving into place. You can lower your larynx without your tongue retracting simply by taking an inhalation while imagining the feeling of an open throat.

### "ARTIFICIAL" CHARACTER SOUNDS

Singers wishing for darker, richer, and fuller voices will often pull their tongues back in an effort to achieve their desired sound. The problem is, an "artificially" dark tone quality usually results. This creates a resonance illusion to the singer's ears that often ends up sounding like a character voice to the audience. In other words, the singer thinks that their voice sounds warm and deep, but the audience hears it as muffled, hollow, or perhaps put on. There is nothing inherently wrong with doing this, and there certainly might be occasions when a character voice is wanted. However, tongue retraction is rarely the best strategy when working towards our most authentic sounds.

### TONGUE TENSION

Finally, tongue retraction can occur as a response to excessive breath pressure. As we've seen, singing relies on a small, steady stream of breath. When breath support fails to provide this from below the vocal folds, the tongue sometimes compensates by holding back the breath from above. Many singers describe this feeling as a kind of "tongue tension."

So, is there light at the end of the tunnel? Absolutely! Thankfully, the tongue is quite easy to see and reposition. As you practice, observe your tongue. Make sure that it is not retracting in an effort to depress your larynx, darken your sound, or hold back undesired breath pressure.

If it is depressing your larynx, see if you can achieve a low and open larynx while keeping your tongue relaxed and stationary. If your sound is coming out artificially dark, then experiment with brighter sounds until you find a better balance. Finally, if your tongue is getting tight because you've been pushing too much volume and vocal weight, then try singing in softer and lighter ways to help your tongue stay put.

*To sing like never before*, we must consider which spaces are worth exploring and which to avoid. Despite the tongue's spelunking skills, it should almost always KEEP OUT of the pharynx. After all, the emptier the cave, the better the echo!

---

  **1** Make sure that your larynx isn't being forced downwards by tongue retraction when you sing.  **2** Artificially dark sounds made by the tongue can obscure your most authentic resonance.  **3** Observe your tongue to ensure that it isn't retracting to hold back excessive breath force.

# WHAT DO KERMIT THE FROG, MARVIN THE MARTIAN, DUDLEY DO-RIGHT AND A GARRULOUS GAGGLE OF GERMAN TENORS HAVE IN COMMON?

# THEIR LOVE OF DUMPLINGS? PERHAPS!

Regrettably, the extent to which any of these individuals enjoy tiny pastry balls is unclear. What is clear, though, is that they all enjoy the "KNURDLE."

**KNURDLE** from the German *knödel*, means "dumpling." In singing, this term originated from the fact that it sounds and feels as though a dumpling is lodged in the throat whenever the tongue squeezes.

*Tongue squeezing* occurs when the hyoglossus muscle contracts during vocal production. Like many muscles, the hyoglossus is named for its anatomical attachments: hyo- (hyoid) and glossus (tongue). Its function is to bring the hyoid bone and the base of the tongue together for swallowing.

Whereas tongue retraction forces the larynx downwards, tongue squeezing brings the larynx upwards. And instead of the artificially deep sound created by tongue retraction, tongue squeezing creates a particularly affected sound known for its theatrical, comedic, or even cartoony qualities.

Unless it is being used for deliberate effect, tongue squeezing is generally a compensation for a lack of strength at the vocal fold level. Most singers have difficulty maintaining vocal fold compression as pitches ascend. So, the larynx becomes elevated in various compensatory ways (like tongue squeezing) to reinforce the solidness and strength that a raised larynx naturally gives.

Tongue squeezing can also indicate poor breath management. Similar to tongue retraction, when breath is not managed properly from beneath the larynx, something often has to counteract it from above. In this case, the tongue and the larynx squeeze together to help resist the air. So, anytime excessive breath pressure is used, there is an increased likelihood that the tongue will get involved.

Interestingly, these habits usually aren't best observed by viewing the tongue itself. The only change to the tongue's outward appearance during tongue squeezing is an occasional curling at its sides. Instead, a sort of bulging is felt and seen in the neck just above the larynx—almost as though a dumpling got stuck there!

Tongue squeezing can usually be solved simply by awareness. Whenever the tongue feels tight or squeezed, try to consciously soften the area. If it persists, try stretching the tongue out of the mouth to relieve any excessive tension. Additionally, vocalizing with the NG consonant can also work wonders as a solution for tongue squeezing.

**To sing like never before**, the knurdle should never be a hurdle. Just be extra cautious the next time you sit down for a nice plate of dumplings. One little slipup and your tongue could be doomed forever!

---

**SLNB QUICK TIPS**

**1** Experience the knurdle by squeezing your tongue's base. This should create a cartoony voice.

**2** Unintentional tongue squeezing is often a byproduct of too little compression or too much air.

**3** Solve tongue squeezing by consciously softening the tongue, stretching it, or using the NG.

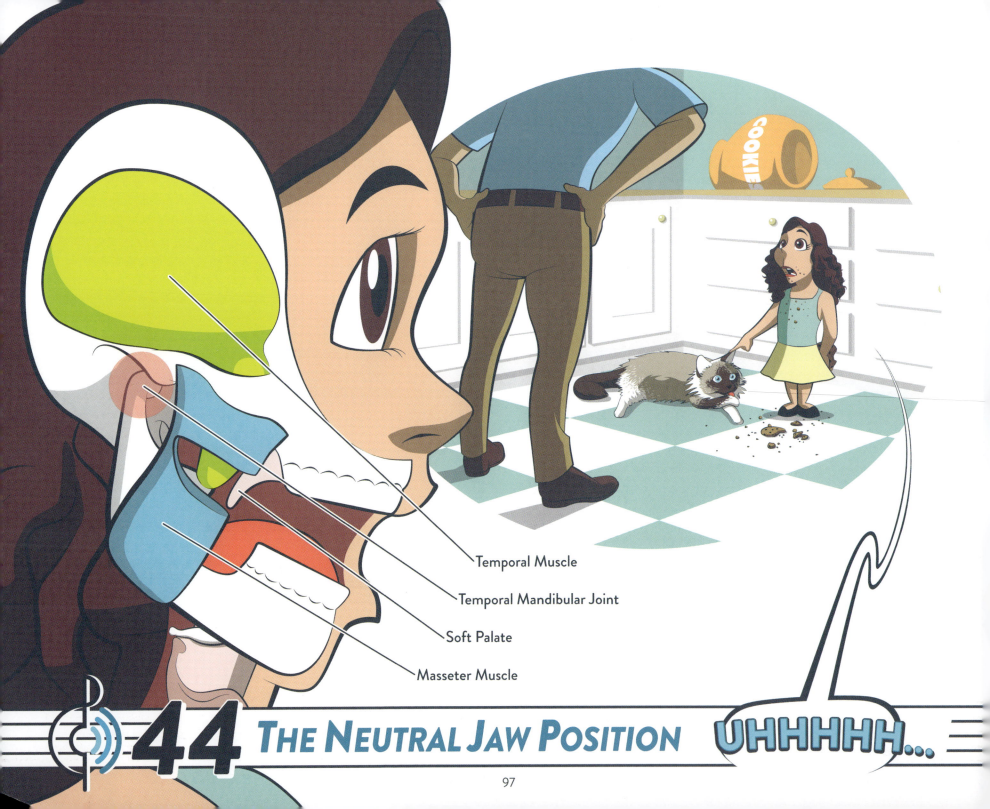

The cookie jar is empty and you have crumbs all over your shirt.

 WHO ATE THESE?!

There's only one guilty answer:

 UHHHHH...

Pop Quiz!

 What are the names of the primary intrinsic larynx muscles?

There's only one head-scratching answer:

 UHHHHH...

Your dentist finishes your last novocaine shot before pulling your bad tooth.

HOW ARE YOU FEELING?

There's only one drooling answer:

UHHHHH...

None of these moments are...

 UHHHHH...

"IDEAL."

But, at least your **JAW POSITION** is!

---

The **NEUTRAL JAW POSITION** is a relaxed "down and back" jaw posture that optimizes vocal freedom and resonance. Historically, this has been termed *raccogliere la bocca*—which means to "collect or gather the mouth" in Italian. To discover the neutral jaw position, drop your jaw subtly, but without yanking it too far down. Instead, let your mouth open comfortably while your jaw moves slightly backwards. Another way to find this position is simply by speaking an UH vowel.

Many people (not just singers) struggle with jaw issues. These can be caused by stress, anxiety, neck and shoulder tension, and alignment problems. Sometimes jaw tension can even manifest itself as temporal mandibular disorder (TMD), which is pain, clicking, or stiffness of the temporal mandibular joint (TMJ).

Jaw tension not only causes pain and discomfort, but it can also inhibit the flexibility, range of motion, and articulatory abilities that singing requires. Biting and chewing muscles like the masseter and temporal muscles are usually responsible for these restrictions. To combat this, try massaging and stretching your jaw muscles on the sides of your cheeks during vocal practice. This will allow your jaw to release into the neutral jaw position and your mouth to open more freely.

On the other hand, some singers tend to open their mouths too far. When this happens, muscles like the digastrics, geniohyoids, and mylohyoids engage to bring the jaw downwards and the larynx upwards. If excessive jaw opening is an unconscious habit, it might be a symptom of singing with too much breath pressure, volume, or weighty vocal registration.

As a solution to your mouth being too open or too closed, try maintaining a neutral jaw position as you move through your range. Be especially vigilant as pitches ascend. This will encourage more freedom in the larynx as well as better resonance in the pharynx and head. You should find that keeping your jaw neutral and free from tension is one of the best ways to create a balanced tone, blended registration, and sustainable vocal technique. Once the neutral jaw position becomes an easy task for you, you can alter it slightly to change up the style or sound.

**To sing like never before**, it's never a great idea for the jaw to be clenched closed or wrenched wide. But, if you ever forget how to find the ideal jaw position, don't think too hard. You already know the answer, right? "UHHHHH..."

---

**1** Find your neutral jaw position by speaking an UH vowel as your jaw releases down and back.

**2** Massage or stretch your jaw muscles if your jaw feels tight or can't open in a relaxed way.

**3** Try keeping a neutral jaw position throughout your range to minimize jaw and larynx tension.

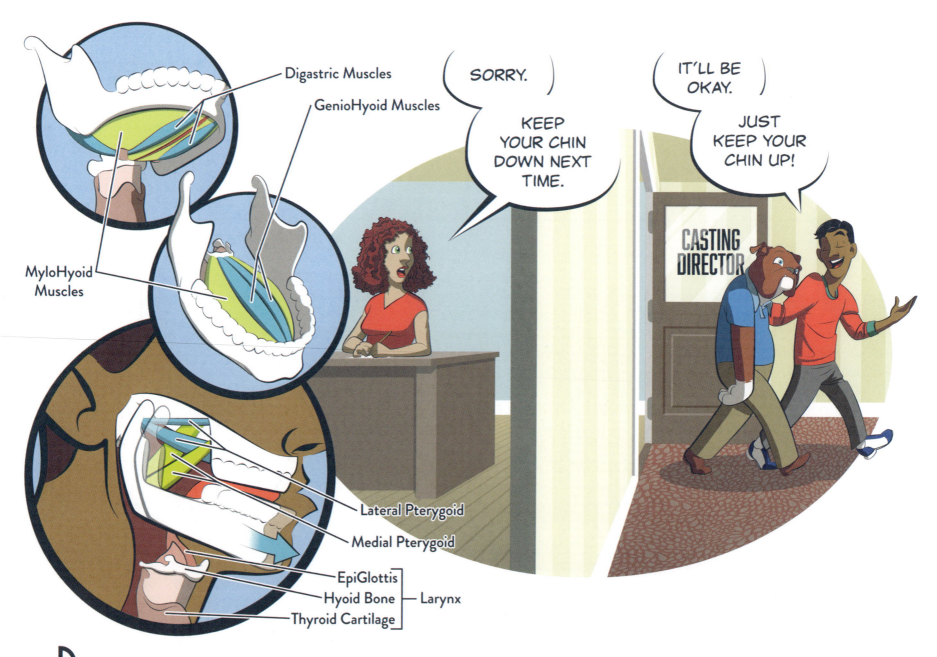

## JAW THRUSTING

**JAW THRUSTING** occurs when the mandible (jaw bone) is brought forward beyond its neutral position by the lateral and medial pterygoid muscles. Jaw thrusting is one of the most common vocal habits and can be particularly problematic in terms of tension, resonance, and alignment.

### TENSION

Jaw thrusting doesn't inherently cause tension. Rather, it is an indicator of tension. It typically occurs to accommodate or make room for tension in the neck, larynx, tongue, and jaw floor muscles. In other words, jaw thrusting is an external compensation for mechanics that aren't going so well internally.

### RESONANCE

Jaw thrusting often happens when less-than-ideal strategies are used to create a fuller sound. These strategies include aggressive breath pressure, an elevated larynx, and a wide-open mouth position. Thus, jaw thrusting often accompanies the sound being pushed out of the mouth. In contrast, a neutral jaw position encourages more ideal resonances in the head and pharynx and minimizes the tendency to push.

### ALIGNMENT

Jaw thrusting can also be symptomatic of posture and alignment issues. As pitches ascend, singers tend to shorten the back of the neck, reach the head forward, and raise the chin. Jaw thrusting frequently leads the way in this process. Consequently, correcting jaw habits is a critical step toward improving posture and alignment.

Thankfully, jaw thrusting is one of the most convenient vocal issues to fix because of its external visibility. Practicing in front of a mirror is a simple and highly effective way to eliminate the problem. This said, jaw thrusting habits are sometimes deeply ingrained. So, be patient with yourself as you work towards a relaxed jaw. If your habits linger, it can be helpful to place a few fingers on the chin during practice. Gentle pressure against the chin instantly reduces jaw thrusting and simultaneously works to improve the alignment of both the head and the neck.

**To sing like never before**, we must keep our chins up without keeping our chins up. So, anytime jaw thrusting tries to sour your singing, just remember: your bark is bigger than your underbite!

---

 **SLNB QUICK TIPS**

**1** Use a mirror to help minimize any jaw thrusting habits in your singing.

**2** Place a finger gently against your chin to discourage excessive jaw thrusting.

**3** Observe the improved resonance, alignment, and freedom that result from a relaxed jaw.

## FROGS REALLY HAVE TALENT!

Have you ever seen their surprising swelling skills? Some frogs swell up to be more alluring to their leggy lovers. Others do it to get some treacherous toad off their territory. Still others just want to croon some old frog folk tune. If you're a frog, you leap at the chance to show off your jaw bulging. But if you're a singer — you'd rather CROAK!

**JAW BULGING** occurs when muscles of the jaw floor contract and push downwards aggressively. This causes a bulky or tense appearance beneath the jaw and above the larynx. If you're noticing tension in these areas, then it's likely the result of jaw bulging.

The three primary muscles involved in jaw bulging are the digastric, mylohyoid, and geniohyoid muscles. The digastric muscle runs from the apex of the jaw to the sides of the hyoid bone and moves the larynx up and forward. It has a second portion that runs from the hyoid to the mastoid process at the back of the head. The *geniohyoid* runs from the jaw's apex to the front of the hyoid bone and also brings the larynx up and forward. The *mylohyoid* runs along the entire floor of the mouth and firms this region. How does all this anatomy help us? Well, it shows us that all three of these muscles:

1. Depress the jaw.
2. Assist with swallowing.
3. Raise the larynx!

That's right—any tension in these muscles is guaranteed to impact your larynx. Remember that your larynx needs to remain fairly free from tension when you sing. So, while jaw bulging may not be a plague of frogs, it's still a habit that can leave your vocal technique a bit soggy. Thankfully, since jaw bulging is fairly easy to observe and to feel, it can be solved in several ways:

**SPACE**—Make sure that your jaw is not causing tension by opening drastically too far. Opt for a gentle down and back opening (i.e. neutral jaw position) whenever possible.

**MOVEMENT**—Move your jaw up and down and side to side mindfully during practice. This will ensure that the jaw floor does not have the opportunity to seize up.

**TOUCH**—Press a finger or two into the underside of the jaw. In most instances, this area should be quite soft and relaxed while you sing. If it's not, then let the pressure from your fingers help you gain awareness of any tension that might be present. From there, let your fingers gently help to calm any unwanted muscular engagement.

**To sing like never before**, the jaw floor should stay soft and supple like a lily pad. If it's bunched and bulky, you probably won't go hoarse, but you'll definitely want that frog out of your throat. So, don't wait any longer to address your jaw tension. Hop to it!

## SLNB QUICK TIPS

1. Use a mirror to ensure that jaw bulging isn't the result of your jaw opening too far.
2. To minimize tension, try moving your jaw up and down and side to side during practice.
3. Gently press your jaw floor with your fingers to ensure that this area remains soft and pliable.

## 47 Jaw / Tongue Separation — PARTNERS IN CRIME

**JAW/TONGUE SEPARATION** is a fundamental vocal skill in which the jaw and tongue articulate freely and independently of each other. Have you ever noticed that vocal exercises are often a lot easier than songs? Or that you can hit a certain note in exercises, but it is more challenging within a song? Perhaps the biggest reason for this is the relationship between the jaw and the tongue.

It is very common for the jaw to tighten unnecessarily or move extraneously during the articulation of consonants. For example, try speaking the G consonant as in the word "go." Say it several times ("GOH-GOH-GOH") and observe what happens. Ideally, the jaw shouldn't move wildly or tense up as the tongue's base articulates the Gs. Instead, the jaw should stay free and relatively still.

Next, try the L consonant by saying "LAH-LAH-LAH." This time the tongue tip articulates instead of the tongue base. Observe again whether there is any jaw movement or tension. If you are achieving jaw/tongue separation, then your tongue tip should be able to perform L consonants independently of the jaw.

We've already seen how jaw and tongue muscles contribute to pressure on the larynx. So, just imagine if every time you performed a certain consonant or word, your voice tightened up. This explains why we sometimes can hit notes in vocal exercises only to find these same notes elusive in the context of a song. When you consider how many times song lyrics tempt your jaw and tongue into teaming up... it's practically criminal!

Thankfully, vocal crime can be fought with articulation exercises! One of the best strategies is to alternate between consonants produced with the tongue tip (i.e. N, L, T, and D) and the tongue base (i.e. NG, Y, K, and G). Alternating between these consonants helps to isolate, practice, and master jaw/tongue separation. Some strange-sounding combinations will result (i.e. NAH-GAH-NAH-GAH, KOH-LOH-KOH-LOH, etc.). However, the goal is to keep your tongue flexible, active, and agile while your jaw stays as relaxed as possible. Once you've mastered this in exercises, the same articulatory freedom is easily applied to songs. You should instantly notice that words are easier to say and notes are more effortless to sing as a result.

**To sing like never before**, the jaw and tongue must not be in cahoots! If we can disassociate this duplicitous duo, then they'll once again become upstanding citizens of the vocal community. In the meantime, though, we'll be watching their every movement...

**1** Try exercises that use the tongue base (i.e. NG, K, Y, G) to ensure that the jaw doesn't move.

**2** Try exercises that use the tongue tip (i.e. N, T, L, D) to again ensure that the jaw doesn't move.

**3** All songs become easier when consonants are free from extraneous movement or tension.

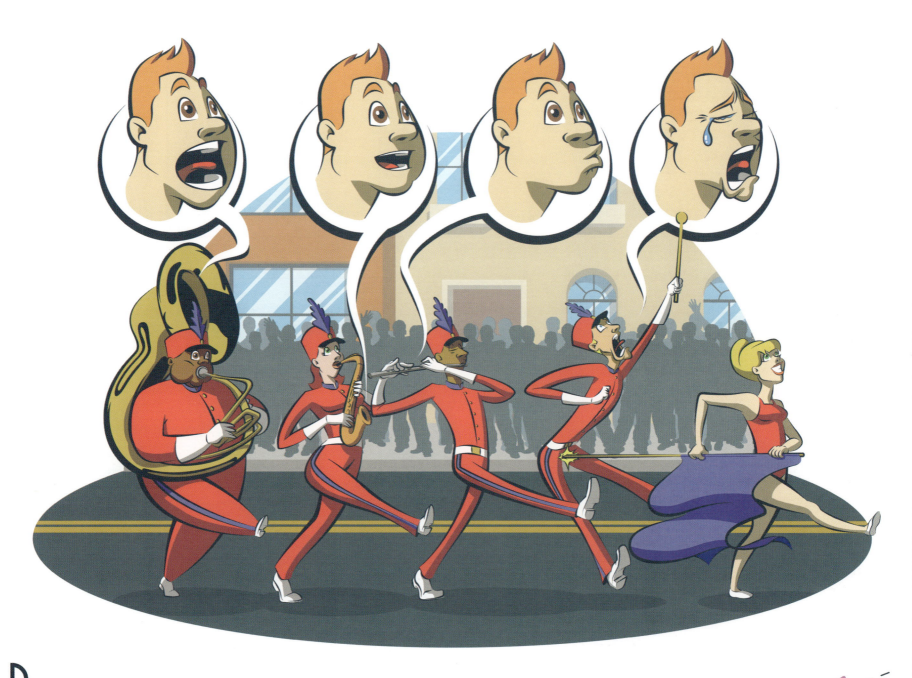

## 48 Jaw Embouchure

**EMBOUCHURE** is a term that describes the position of the jaw, tongue, and lips. It usually refers to the playing of various wind instruments such as woodwinds, flutes, and brass. However, it just so happens that the voice is the ultimate wind instrument!

Much like any wind instrument, the voice receives its pulmonary power from the lungs. However, rather than vibration happening with a reed or mouthpiece, the vocal folds vibrate instead. Similarly, the position of the jaw, tongue, and lips alter the resonance and function of our vocal wind instrument, just like they would any other instrument. Let's begin with jaw embouchure...

*Jaw embouchure* is the position of the jaw during singing. The jaw's position correlates directly with the strength or flexibility of the voice. Opening the jaw (like during an AH vowel) increases mouth space and raises the first formant (F1), which generally strengthens the voice. Closing the jaw (like during an OO vowel) lowers F1, which tends to increase vocal flexibility.

As pitches ascend, opening the jaw embouchure helps in maintaining or "dragging up" vocal registers. In other words, if we wish to maintain strength in our chest voice or head voice on higher notes, then one way is to enlarge the mouth space. This can be handy on occasion, but it is questionable to use this strategy too frequently. Opening the jaw embouchure is often accompanied by more breath pressure, more volume, and an unwanted raised larynx. While vocal strength is certainly boosted, it also comes with the possibility of a loss of control and ease.

Ideally, we should seek to balance strength and flexibility in our voices. So, if your jaw embouchure is consistently too open or too closed, you may find your voice skewed in one direction or another. As a first step, try keeping your jaw embouchure neutral and unchanging as pitches move. This will establish the conditions for your most optimal vocal technique. If you start with this discipline from a technical standpoint, then jaw embouchure adjustments can later be added for stylistic and acoustical purposes.

**To sing like never before**, mastering embouchure isn't minor—it's MAJOR. That's why that highfalutin' drum major can go and toot his own horn. Because even if you never play a single note, you'll always have the best wind instrument around!

**1** Explore your jaw embouchure to find a position that feels neither too closed nor too open.

**2** Experiment with opening your jaw embouchure to encourage vocal strength.

**3** Experiment with closing your jaw embouchure to encourage vocal flexibility.

**TONGUE EMBOUCHURE** is the position of the tongue during singing. We all speak in our native tongue without thinking twice. Yet, the endless variety of languages, accents, and sounds that humans can produce is made possible largely through alterations to the tongue's placement. In fact, every vowel has its own unique tongue embouchure.

First, let's look at the tongue's front-to-back movement. The *genioglossus* extends the tongue, while the *styloglossus* retracts it. As the tongue moves out of the mouth, the sound generally gets brighter as F2 rises. *Formant 2* (F2) corresponds primarily with the brightness or darkness of a vowel.

To experience this, try saying the AA vowel (as in "bad cat"). Begin with your tongue in your mouth and then extend it outwards as you say each word. (Watch out for mischievous kitties when you do this!). You'll notice that as your tongue exits your mouth, your resonance gets brighter (F2 rises).

Contrast this with the ER vowel (as in "bird"), which retracts the tongue. You'll notice that your resonance gets darker (F2 lowers). Alternate between the words "cat" and "bird" to experience the stark resonance differences between these two tongue embouchures.

Next, let's examine the tongue's up-and-down movement. The *palatoglossus* lifts the base of the tongue, while the *hyoglossus* depresses it. As the tongue's base moves upwards (like the EE vowel), space in the mouth decreases and the pharynx is less impeded by the tongue. As a result, the voice gets brighter (F2 rises) and more flexible (F1 lowers). Conversely, as the tongue's base moves downwards (like the AH vowel), mouth space increases and the pharynx is more impeded by the tongue's base. Consequently, the voice gets darker (F2 lowers) and stronger (F1 rises).

So, what do we do with all of this as singers? Well, let's not pussyfoot around the matter! Generally speaking, tongue embouchure can be made as simple as this:

- Fronting your tongue will make your voice brighter.
- Retracting your tongue will make your voice darker.
- Raising your tongue's base will increase both brightness and flexibility.
- Lowering your tongue's base will increase both darkness and strength.

**To sing like never before**, curiosity won't kill you, but an untamed tongue just might. So, allow your tongue to explore the whole kit and caboodle of resonance possibilities. If you do, then your voice will truly be the cat's meow!

 Experiment with various tongue positions and compare the changes in resonance that result.

 As you practice, observe your tongue's tendencies. Does it gravitate toward a certain position?

 Even if your tongue has preferences, make sure that it ultimately remains loose and adaptable.

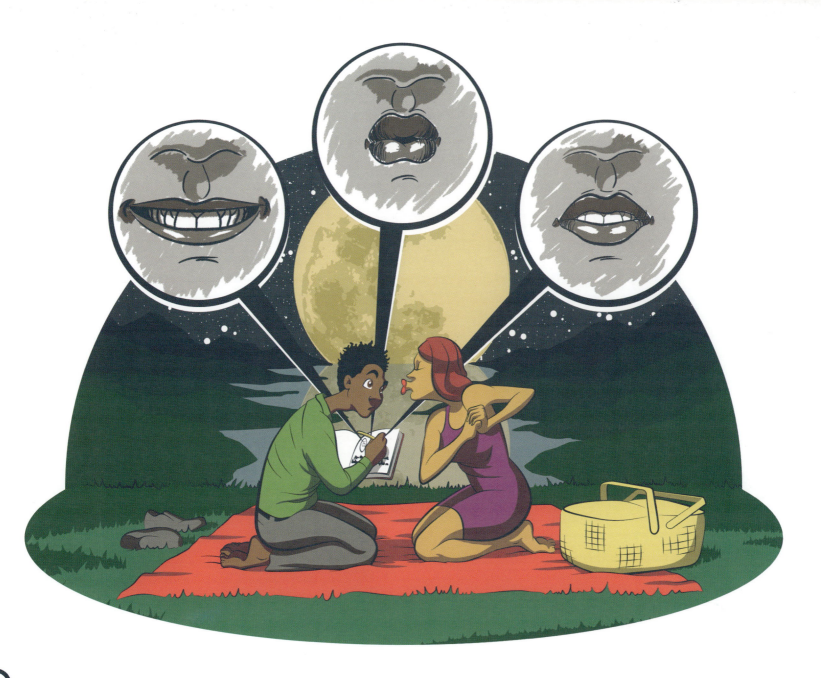

# 50 Lip Embouchure — Lips' Service

It's a balmy August evening.
The moon sparkles. The water glistens. Your eyes meet.
Your date's lips blossom from a coy pout into an inviting SMILE.
Before you know it, these same eager lips pucker up for a KISS.
Yet, you just stare... You forget to kiss back....
Why? Because you're a singer! All you can think about is the impressive array of Lip Embouchures that you've just witnessed! Your date SNARLS and storms off.

But you're still smiling!

**LIP EMBOUCHURE** is the position of the lips during singing. Just like jaw embouchure and tongue embouchure, the lips directly impact vocal resonance. This occurs most noticeably through spreading, puckering, and snarling.

## SPREADING

Spreading occurs when the lip corners move away from the center of the mouth, like in a smile. This strengthens and brightens the voice (F1 and F2 rise). Spreading is occasionally desirable for modifying vowels or creating a brighter vocal tone. However, it's also one of the worst and most common vocal habits. Singers who spread too much for high notes often have the tendency to push air and volume as pitches ascend. They also have a more difficult time finding their more ideal resonance within the vocal tract, since spreading frequently causes the sound to be pushed out the mouth. Simply put: try not to spread your lips unless it is an acoustical choice!

## PUCKERING

Puckering occurs when the lip corners move inward, like in a smooch. Puckering is the opposite of spreading. It darkens the voice and encourages flexibility by lowering F1 and F2. This is usually necessary for lip-rounded vowels such as OO and OH. However, puckering outside the context of lip-rounded vowels creates vocal tone that sounds exaggeratedly dark. So, make sure that your lips are only narrowing for the vowels that require lip-rounding. Otherwise, only use puckering for the times when you are seeking a stylized dark quality.

## SNARLING

Snarling occurs when the upper lip exposes the top teeth—like when you're disgusted with your date. Snarling doesn't alter vocal tone to the same degree as spreading and puckering. However, it does tend to encourage nasal resonance. Although there are no direct muscle pairs between the lips and the soft palate, many singers experience a strong connection between snarling and nasal resonance. If you are seeking more nasal resonance in your voice, snarling can be a helpful way to find it.

**To sing like never before**, we must never pay lip service to embouchure. Our first task is to navigate our vocal ranges with as few embouchure adjustments as possible. Once we've achieved this, any alterations to jaw, tongue, and lip embouchures become the basis for modifying vowels and for most acoustical decisions. As our technique progresses, almost all embouchures can be the perfect choice to suit any mood or occasion. How romantic...

**1** Try singing with a spread embouchure. You should notice a brighter and stronger tone.

**2** Then sing with a puckered embouchure. You should notice a darker and more flexible tone.

**3** Finally, sing with a snarled embouchure. In many cases, this encourages nasal resonance.

# CHAPTER 6
*VOCAL REGISTRATION*

# ON THE 8TH DAY GOD WOKE UP, YAWNED, AND STRETCHED.

And God called them all "**GOOD**." Yet, mankind has not the ears of God. So, alas, mankind stubbornly labelled **VOCAL REGISTERS** of its own free will. And to the present day, mankind liveth in remorse for this decision.

**VOCAL REGISTRATION** is the categorization of vibratory changes (primary) and qualitative changes (secondary) that occur across a singer's vocal range. Vocal registers have historically received countless titles such as:

Head, Chest, Mix, Voix Mixte, Fry, Pulse, Thyroarytenoid Dominant, Cricothyroid Dominant, Falsetto, Flageolet, Heavy Mechanism, Light Mechanism, Belt, Whistle, Modal, Creak, M1, M2... and many more!

However, the reality is: vocal registration (as perceived and described by singers and voice teachers) has never been an exact science. Consequently, vocal registration has remained one of the most debated, divisive, and controversial topics in the vocal community for generations. Even today, there is still no universal consensus nor standard terminology for labeling vocal registers.

Scientifically speaking, vocal registration is mostly determined by measuring the vibratory function of the vocal folds. *Closed quotient* is the duration of time that the vocal folds stay closed during their vibratory cycle. Stronger (chestier) registers result from vocal folds that remain closed for longer periods during their vibratory cycle, while more flexible (headier) registers have lower closed quotients.

This said, vibratory function isn't the sole determining factor for vocal registers. Variations in breath, larynx position, vocal fold length, vocal fold compression, resonance, and embouchure also impact vocal registration.

A further complexity stems from the fact that listeners' aural observations and singers' physical sensations also contribute to how vocal registers become labelled, defined, or described. So, how many vocal registers are there?

In a certain sense, vocal registration is actually infinite. In other words, if mankind had the ears of God, then every single minuscule mechanical change to vibratory function and resonance quality could theoretically be observed and labelled. The result would be endless vocal registers! While the vastness of this is fun to consider, the complexity is overwhelming.

For this reason, labels like the many examples listed above remain essential for describing, communicating, and mastering the endless possibilities of the singing voice. The secret is to not become dogmatic, but rather to use vocal register labels only insofar as they are practical and beneficial. In the coming chapter, we will explore and define some of the most common terminology for vocal registration. From this standpoint, we will seek to have a tangible (yet highly adaptable) vocabulary to communicate the most significant vocal registration events that occur in all of our voices.

**To sing like never before**, vocal registration shouldn't cause any weeping or gnashing of teeth. That's why we must always stay open-minded, collaborative, and communicative when exploring vocal registration. In the process, we hope that infinity starts to become a bit more down to Earth. If that's the case, then we can truly say... **HALLELUJAH!**

---

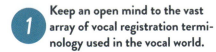
Keep an open mind to the vast array of vocal registration terminology used in the vocal world.

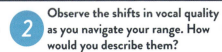
Observe the shifts in vocal quality as you navigate your range. How would you describe them?

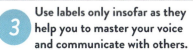
Use labels only insofar as they help you to master your voice and communicate with others.

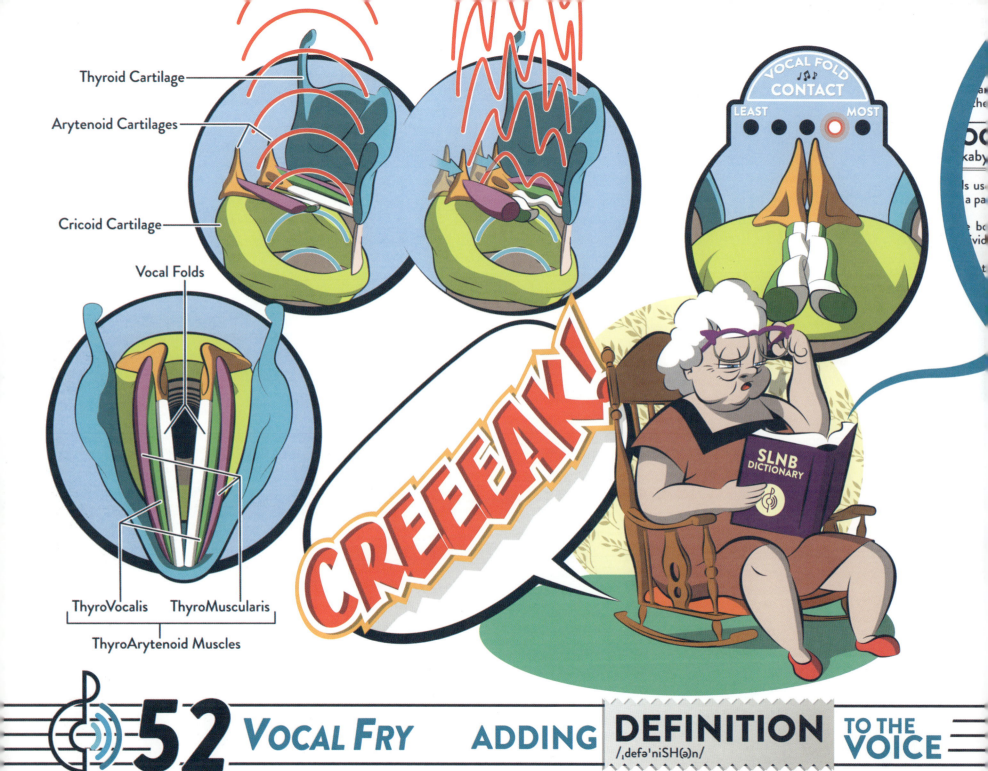

## VOCAL FRY
/ˈvōk(ə)l/ /frī/

① *noun*
A sound used exclusively by teenagers, former US Presidents, and Elmer Fudd.

*nope!*

② *verb*
To sing outdoors in sweltering heat.

*wrong again!*

③ *verb*
To cook the vocal folds in oil until crispy golden brown.

*strike three!*

# SO, WHAT IS THE REAL DEFINITION?

**VOCAL FRY** is the lowest vocal register and is distinguished by its creaking quality. It occurs when the vocal folds are shortened by thyroarytenoid (thyromuscularis) and very lightly compressed by vocalis (thyrovocalis) and other adduction muscles. Ordinarily, our ranges stop when we reach our lowest chest voice notes. The vocal folds shorten and slacken so much that phonation ceases. However, adduction muscles compensate for this beneath the chest voice to create the vocal fry register.

Fry is often misunderstood to be damaging. While it can certainly be a poor habit for the speaking voice, vocal fry is actually quite healthy, as it is a natural part of our instrument. In fact, vocal fry is frequently used as a tool for improving overall vocal technique, and even for vocal rehabilitation in some cases.

To find your vocal fry, start by singing the lowest note in your range and then going even a little lower. At the same time, allow your voice to naturally transition into a creaky or popping quality. Most of the time these creaks and pops are irregular, and even erratic. However, some singers develop their vocal fry into reliable extensions beneath their lowest chest voice notes. Vocal fry qualities can also be taken up into other higher registers of the voice as both technical and stylistic tools.

One of vocal fry's largest benefits is that it requires minimal airflow. Singers often struggle to navigate their ranges due to their voice's all or nothing tendencies. Pushing chest voice too high results in a shouty, bombastic, or forced quality. Alternatively, switching to head voice or falsetto too low results in a disconnected, aspirate, or weak quality. It can be quite challenging to maintain subtle amounts of vocal fold compression as pitches ascend without relying on breath or volume. Vocal fry can help with this problem!

Vocal fry always requires light vocal fold compression coupled with small amounts of breath force. Thus, doing vocal exercises that involve vocal fry in some way can encourage coordinated amounts of definition throughout your upper range and the transitional areas of your voice. Don't be afraid to experiment with a little vocal fry within your technique practice.

Vocal fry can also be used stylistically and is a very common feature of contemporary singing. It's used frequently as an onset at the beginnings of words—especially those starting with vowels. It can also create a contrasting texture when incorporated alongside aspirate (breathy) phonation and clean phonation. Finally, vocal fry's dysphonic qualities are sometimes used as rasp and distortion elements in some vocal styles.

**To sing like never before**, your voice probably doesn't need a dictionary. But, it does need the definition that can only be provided by a certain three-letter word!

---

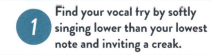

**1** Find your vocal fry by softly singing lower than your lowest note and inviting a creak.

**2** Use vocal fry to practice both light compression and small breath force in your upper range.

**3** Experiment with vocal fry as a stylistic tool to occasionally add texture, emotion, or distortion.

# CHEST VOICE CAN BE CONFUSING.

**IF YOU COMPLIMENT A MAN ON HIS 'NICE CHEST,' HE'LL PROBABLY GLANCE DOWN, PUFF HIMSELF UP, AND SAY:** *THANKS! YOU SHOULD SEE HOW MUCH I CAN BENCH PRESS!*

**BUT, IF YOU COMPLIMENT HIM ON HIS 'NICE THYROARYTENOID DOMINANCE,' YOU'LL PROBABLY GET A MUCH MORE BEWILDERED RESPONSE:** *UH... THANKS... I... HARDLY EVEN WORK OUT...*

**CHEST VOICE** (M1) is the most commonly used vocal register because it is found in most people's everyday speaking voices. Interestingly though, chest voice doesn't have very much to do with the chest itself. In fact, it has much more to do with the thyroarytenoid muscle.

As we've seen, the thyroarytenoid is used to shorten and thicken our vocal folds. When this happens, both vocal fold mass and closed quotient can increase. This creates the possibility for more vocal strength in both the speaking voice and singing voice.

In speech, chest voice exists naturally in low and middle speaking ranges relative to each person. When brought higher in pitch and volume, chest voice turns into shouting, yelling, or highly-projected speech.

In singing, chest voice is used primarily for low, middle, and occasionally upper-middle notes. When carried to higher notes, very heavy and loud vocal sounds usually result. While this can be impressive at times, it isn't advisable for your vocal health to do on a consistent basis. A much more sustainable approach is to allow vocal registers to transition to lighter registers like mix voice and head voice as pitches ascend. We'll explore these throughout this chapter.

So, why was it ever called chest voice in the first place? The answer stems from the fact that we really feel it in our chests. Give it a try! Place a hand on your chest and call out a bold "HEY!" You probably feel some chesty vibrations. However, the chest isn't what makes the sound. So what's the deal? The answer is found in exploring the differences between sympathetic resonance vs. conductive resonance.

*Sympathetic resonance* refers to the way sound waves resonate inside the open spaces of the vocal tract. As sound moves through these open spaces, they respond and adjust to (sympathize with) changes made to the vocal tract (position of the larynx, jaw, tongue, lips, soft palate, etc.). *Conductive resonance* refers to the vibratory impact the vocal folds and breath have on surrounding surfaces like the chest, neck, cheeks, sinuses, and forehead. Here's a good way to remember it:

- Sympathetic resonance is what the audience *hears*.
- Conductive resonance is what the singer *feels*.

**To sing like never before**, we need to know our own strength. While we may *feel* chest voice in our chests, it's important to know that its source actually lies inside the vocal folds. So, the next time someone compliments you on your "nice chest!"—just remind them that true strength comes from within!

---

**SLNB QUICK TIPS**

1. Place a hand on your chest and speak a bold "HEY!" You will likely feel chest vibrations.
2. Work on developing your chest voice to ensure that your voice has reliable vocal strength.
3. Avoid taking chest voice too high too often (i.e. yelling). Adjust to lighter registers instead.

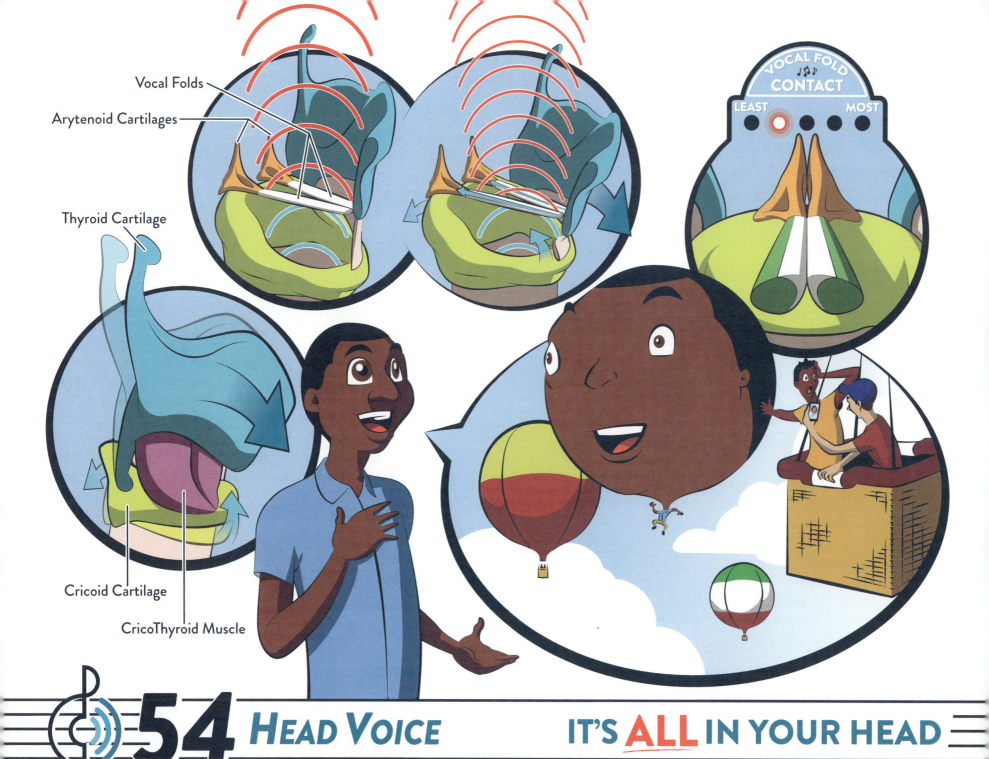

 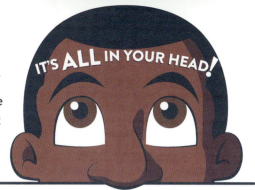

**HEAD VOICE** (M2) refers to the upper registers of the voice. Just like chest voice, head voice has also been associated with a wide variety of terminology—"cricothyroid dominant production," "light mechanism," "loft," etc. Head voice involves lengthening the vocal folds via the cricothyroid muscle while also diminishing much of their thickness and mass. This makes higher pitches easier and also possible. To achieve these higher pitches, the vocal folds lengthen, decrease in contact, and increase in open quotient.

Head voice has a much lighter vocal quality than chest voice. Yet, head voice is not necessarily aspirate or breathy. Even though it can be thought of as our vocal flexibility, it actually has the potential for quite a bit of strength. However, its strength differs vastly from that of chest voice. Chest voice's strength relies predominantly on its greater presence of vocal fold mass. In contrast, head voice's strength relies on resonance tuning, embouchure adjustments, vocal fold approximation, and the inherent carrying power of higher frequencies.

Historically, the term "head voice" has been applied differently to males and females. The traditional female head voice is a production that is truly distinct from chest voice. In other words, female head voice disconnects or breaks from chest voice (M1) as pitches ascend into a distinctively thinner (M2) production.

The traditional male head voice is actually a blended vocal register (mix voice) that *does* connect with chest voice. In other words, male head voice is a light variety of chest voice (M1). The male M2 that is distinct from chest voice (M1) has historically been called "falsetto." Thus, male head voice is still a kind of mix, or M1, whereas "falsetto" is the term most commonly used for male M2.

So, with all of these confusing distinctions—why was it ever called head voice to begin with? The answer is again found in exploring sympathetic resonance vs. conductive resonance. When the cricothyroid lengthens the vocal folds, conductive resonance is usually felt more acutely throughout the head and face. Try it! Go ahead and call out a high pitched "WOO!" Likely you felt the sound in the back of your head, top of your head, or in the front of your face.

We already know that all vocal sounds resonate sympathetically in the head. So, in a certain sense, it seems like *everything* should be called head voice. But again, we see that vocal terminology has historically favored physical sensations above technical specificity. Nevertheless, these sensations are not invalid. You might indeed find visualizing high notes "upwards into the head" to be a helpful tool for mastering your upper range.

**To sing like never before**, high notes mustn't mystify your mind. After all, you now understand both the history and the physiology of head voice. Swell! Just don't let it go to your head!

  Try a high-pitched "WOO!" You might feel conductive resonance in your head, cheeks, or face.  Practice head voice consistently to help your voice to stay flexible, agile, and healthy.  Experiment with visualizing the sound traveling upwards into your head on higher notes.

If you're baking cookies, then don't do it on an empty stomach. Otherwise, you might be tempted to eat some of the ingredients ahead of time. Problem is - none of them taste right by themselves. Sure, the milk's mostly manageable and the sugar's sorta sweet. But, the **RAW EGGS** are **REPULSIVE**! The **FLOUR** is **FOUL**!! And the **BAKING SODA** is **BARFABLE**!!!

You see - baking is just like singing: you have to  the ingredients together to get it right...

**MIX VOICE** is not a singular vocal register, but rather an endless smorgasbord of potential muscular coordinations and resonances. The term originates from the French "*voix mixte.*" In contemporary singing, mix voice can have a broad range of applications and meanings. We've just seen that chest voice predominates in lower ranges, while head voice extends into upper ranges. Mix voice, though, thrives *in between* these two registers. To do so, it requires two main ingredients:

### PRIMARY INGREDIENT—MUSCLE COORDINATIONS
Mix voice is a balancing act between the lengthening and thickening muscles of the vocal folds. While there could be endless mix voice coordinations, let's take a look at two of the most common varieties—chest dominant mix and head dominant mix.

**CHEST DOMINANT MIX** refers to register coordinations that lengthen the vocal folds with the cricothyroid while maintaining ample compression and thickness from the thyroarytenoid and the adduction muscles. You might describe this sound as strong or "belty," yet without getting too loud or pressed.

**HEAD DOMINANT MIX** refers to register coordinations that are also lengthened by the cricothyroid, but with noticeably less compression and thickness. This sound might be described as light or "floaty," yet with still enough substance to prevent it from being perceived as a fully head voice or falsetto quality.

### SECONDARY INGREDIENT—RESONANCE
Some resonance gestures tend to lighten mix voice coordinations. Examples include narrowing the embouchure, closing the jaw, or slightly lowering the soft palate. As you try any one of these, notice what effect it has on lightening your vocal registration.

Other resonance gestures tend to strengthen mix voice coordinations. Examples include widening the embouchure, opening the jaw, or elevating the soft palate. As you experiment with these in your voice, you'll likely notice that they help strengthen your vocal registration.

While resonance adjustments like these apply to all vocal registers, they become essential elements of the mix voice because of the balance and precision it requires.

### INFINITE COOKBOOK!
Just like bakers, singers must use different recipes for different stylistic occasions. Chesty qualities in your mix voice can help you sound strong, solid, and full. However, too much of this may sound heavier and thicker than you desire. Heady qualities give your mix voice a lighter, softer, and gentler quality. But, too much of this may be weaker or thinner than you want.

One of the best things that you can do to improve your singing is to explore as many in-between coordinations as possible. Experiment with different amounts of compression and volume as well as many resonance strategies. If you do, then you'll eventually become a master chef when it comes to your voice's many recipes.

**To sing like never before**, we need to find balance no matter how the cookie crumbles. So, don't just gorge yourself on one sound or another. Instead, blend your resonance and registration in all the ways that you can cook up. After all, variety is the spice of vocal life!

 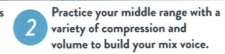

1. Experiment with various recipes that combine ingredients of chest voice and head voice.
2. Practice your middle range with a variety of compression and volume to build your mix voice.
3. Explore how changes in resonance can either strengthen or lighten your vocal registers.

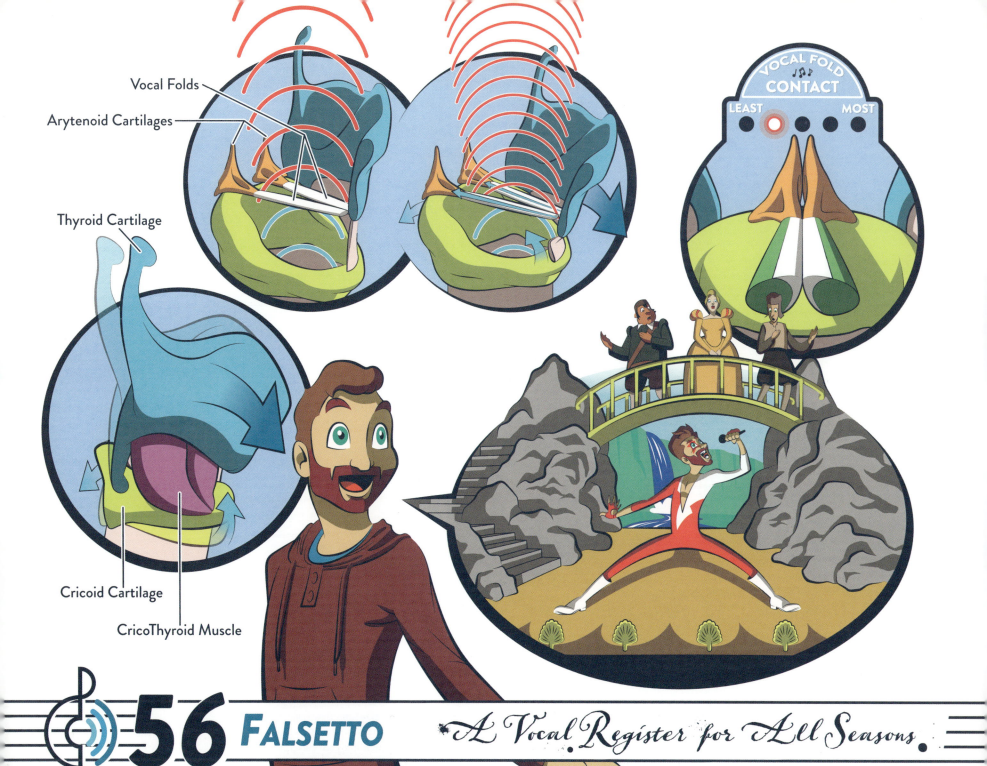

*Man, how times change! In the 17th Century, gender norms were quite different than they are today. A man who sang "like a lady" was sometimes considered "FALSE." Today though, a man who sings "like a lady" might be considered a pop icon. Yet, despite our societal progress, "TrueSetto" has never caught on as a vocal register. We still say that modern males sing in "Falsetto!"*

**FALSETTO** is a term historically used to describe the higher, thinner vocal register (M2) in male voices. Falsetto involves lengthened vocal folds that are disengaged from much of the thickness and compression found in lower registers like chest voice and mix voice. Thus, it possesses a far higher degree of open quotient than these lower vocal registers. This is what gives falsetto its lighter quality.

What is sometimes labelled "male head voice" is actually different from falsetto. While male head voice involves the same kind of lengthening of the vocal folds that we see in falsetto, it still incorporates enough thickness and presence from the compression muscles to make a seamless transition into chest voice. In this sense, what people often label "male head voice" could also be described as a light mix voice or light M1 coordination.

Falsetto, on the other hand, does not make this same seamless transition (at least not without training and practice). Since it is an M2 event, it will naturally crack back (abruptly reconnect) into lower vocal registers. Female head voice (also M2) similarly lacks this ability to transition seamlessly. So, functionally speaking, the terms "male falsetto" and "female head voice" are considered to be equivalent. It is certainly safe to say that they both can be classified as M2 registers.

Still, some may ask: "Is there a female falsetto?" Not really. People ask this question because a breathy or aspirate quality is very common in a male falsetto. So, when this same quality is present in a female head voice, it sometimes gets mislabeled as a "female falsetto." Even though vocal registration terms have never been entirely definitive, most pedagogues do not distinguish a breathy female M2 (female falsetto) as a separate register. The breathiness is merely an added effect. Regardless, it is essential to understand that male falsetto *does not require* breathy or aspirate qualities. Like most vocal registers, falsetto can be done in either a solid or a breathy way. One of the more dramatic examples of a solid falsetto is what is sometimes called "reinforced falsetto."

**REINFORCED FALSETTO** is a variant of falsetto that is specifically *not* aspirate, but rather is quite solid (adducted) and also reinforced by several factors. These include a high larynx position, increased twang and bright resonances, and a widened embouchure. Despite its adduction and powerful ringing resonance, reinforced falsetto is still an M2 coordination. So, without training and practice, it will still naturally crack into thicker vocal registers as the pitch is lowered.

**To sing like never before**, all males must develop their falsetto, just as all females must develop their head voice. Society has certainly evolved over the centuries. So has vocal terminology. Yet, even with its antiquated name, falsetto is still a true and trustworthy path to vocal flexibility… in every season.

  All males should embrace falsetto wholeheartedly and integrate it into daily vocal practice.  When practicing falsetto, make sure that it can be done without necessarily becoming breathy.  Explore your resonance to find that falsetto can become quite strong when it is reinforced.

| But, if you think about it, there's no reason to fear a faultless furry friend - **IT'S JUST A MOUSE!** | In the same way, there's no reason to run from a rather rangy register - **IT'S JUST FLAGEOLET!** |

**FLAGEOLET** (M3) is the highest of all vocal registers in which the vocal folds vibrate in their standard wavelike fashion. Registers that vibrate in non-wavelike ways are vocal fry (which can extend lower than chest voice), and whistle voice (which can extend even higher than flageolet).

The term "flageolet" is a French word that means "small flute." So, you can also call flageolet—"flute voice." But, don't get flageolet and whistle voice mixed up. They are indeed two distinct registers. The reason they get confused is that they are both very high-pitched "flutey" and "whistly" sounds at the extreme top of the voice. But, as we will see in the next section, whistle voice brings the vocal folds *together* to create its sound, whereas flageolet brings the vocal folds *apart*. Still, with two neighboring registers named after tiny wind instruments, you can once again see why vocal registers get so confusing!

Both males and females can access flageolet. For males, flageolet can be thought of as the "falsetto above falsetto." For females, flageolet is simply the "head voice above head voice." Here are some characteristics of flageolet:

- It often has a very squeaky quality.
- The vocal folds stretch to their lengthiest capabilities.
- The vocal folds make either no contact or almost no contact, making the open quotient higher than any of the vocal registers. This is the most distinctive element of flageolet.
- When discovering flageolet, breath force and volume should ideally be kept at an absolute minimum to encourage the lightest vibrations possible.
- Decompression (breathiness/aspirate sounds) can help in the development of flageolet by ensuring that the vocal folds don't make too much contact.
- Resonance tuning using head dominant vowels (OO and EE), approximants (especially W), nasal consonants (M, N, NG), and trills (lip and tongue) encourage flageolet the most.

All of these factors combine to help us sing notes at the highest part of our voices. Many of these notes vibrate at least one thousand times per second. For example, most females (and some males) can sing C6 in flageolet. C6 vibrates around 1,050 times per second. Some females may even be able to sing past C7, which vibrates almost 2,100 times per second!

If you've never experienced flageolet before, you can begin to discover it by allowing your voice to break or crack. Everyone is familiar with the sometimes embarrassing crack from chest voice (M1) to head voice (M2). However, this is yet another higher crack. Female singers actually crack out of head voice (M2) into flageolet (M3). Likewise, male singers crack out of falsetto (M2) into flageolet (M3).

*Remember: cracking isn't unhealthy for the voice—it's just the opposite.* It is simply the vocal folds making adjustments toward their lightest vibrational preferences as pitches ascend. If anything, allowing your voice to crack when it is time to crack promotes flexibility in your instrument as opposed to hanging onto vocal weight.

Flageolet isn't often heard in songs, but its benefits for improving vocal technique are boundless. In fact, there is perhaps *no better way to increase vocal range and flexibility* than by building your flageolet. Keep in mind that the same pair of vocal folds do everything in our voices. So, if we've learned to hit the highest possible notes with the least amount of volume and force, every other vocal register will benefit from the flexibility. If you commit to developing your flageolet, you will likely see some dramatic transformations.

Sadly though, flageolet is usually the most neglected vocal register. Singers are often rather unwilling to let their voices crack into flageolet. Or, they are too embarrassed to give it a try because of its inherent squeakiness. This said, any singer who celebrates these sounds will quickly find the very breadcrumbs that pave the path to vocal mastery.

**To sing like never before**, we must change our mentality about flageolet. Don't fear the squeakiness of mice and men. Instead, embrace the mouse within!

**1** To access flageolet, try singing at the highest part of your range on a tiny OO or EE vowel.

**2** One of the biggest secrets to finding flageolet is to welcome its quiet and squeaky nature.

**3** Practicing flageolet is one of the finest ways to increase your vocal range and flexibility.

**WHISTLE VOICE** is the highest vocal register that the human voice can produce. In whistle voice, the vocal folds do not vibrate using their standard mucosal wave. Instead, they become fully taut across their entire length. When small gaps are opened up and air leaks through them, the result is a very high-pitched whistling sound.

So far, we've seen that many vocal registers have unfortunate and sometimes confusing titles. Whistle voice, though, is perhaps the most aptly-named register. This is because whistle voice is essentially whistling with your vocal folds instead of with your lips.

If you can whistle with your lips or teeth, try whistling a tune. What vibrates to create the sound? Nothing! It's simply the sound of air moving through the mouth while pitch is manipulated by the lips, jaw, and tongue. In whistle voice, the air moves through the vocal folds and pitch is manipulated by the intrinsic vocal muscles and the larynx.

Another similarity between whistling and whistle voice is that both can be performed on either an inhale or an exhale. *Inhale phonation* means vocalizing using an inhalation instead of an exhalation. It typically produces a comically creaky sound for most speaking and singing. However, many singers can only discover their whistle voice at first by vocalizing on an inhale and then bringing the vocal folds together in a vocal fry-like gesture. With some practice, this surprising coordination can extend far higher than the flageolet register.

While whistle voice is fascinating, it is notorious for its disproportionate relationship between singers' desire to practice it and its actual usability. In reality, whistle voice has limited value apart from its unusual and exotic aesthetic. It is rarely heard in repertoire and it does very little to improve overall technique and vocal registration. So, while it's certainly not wrong to develop your whistle voice, it should rarely become the focal point of practice sessions.

**To sing like never before**, feel free to explore whistle voice, but don't work like a dog to achieve it. After all, Fido may not be able to resist whistle frequencies. But, for the most part, singers can let sleeping dogs lie!

**Disclaimer:** Always exercise caution when experimenting with whistle voice and inhale phonation. Pain and hoarseness are not okay. Study with a whistle voice specialist for mastery of the skills introduced in this section.

---

**SLNB QUICK TIPS**

1. To discover the beginnings of whistle voice, try a gentle inhale phonation through a vocal fry.
2. Once your vocal folds achieve whistle voice on an inhale, reverse it to a very light exhale.
3. Whistle voice should never be your primary focus, but an occasional curiosity instead.

**A BELT IS SIMPLY** - what keeps your pants from falling down.

**A BELT IS SIMPLY** - a solid smack.

**A BELT IS SIMPLY** - an assembly of asteroids.

**BUT, A BELT IS SIMPLY NOT** - AS SIMPLE AS A SHOUT!

**BELTING** is the extension of specific vocal registers beyond their native range for stylistic effect. The registers most commonly used for belting are chest voice and mix voice (although reinforced falsetto and head voice are sometimes included). Belting also requires resonance tuning adjustments that can make our voices appear bigger, fuller, and perhaps (at times) more shout-like than they actually are.

Belting is an essential skill for virtually all contemporary styles of music. Yet, vocal pedagogy has historically given it an unfair bad rap. A common oversimplification suggests that belting is nothing but shouting and therefore inherently harmful to the voice. In reality, though, belting only becomes a shout when chest voice is dragged upwards with excessive breath pressure and volume. If this is done exclusively or for long durations, then belting can indeed become stressful, fatiguing, and potentially damaging to the vocal folds. Thankfully, belting is not so simple!

As we've seen, all vocal registers possess mechanics that naturally suit a certain range of pitches. As pitches ascend, stronger registers naturally transition to more flexible registers. On higher pitches, the vocal folds instinctively opt for lighter vibrational situations which involve less vocal fold thickness and less closed quotient.

*Belting technique* is the strategic delaying of these thinner vocal fold preferences in favor of thicker productions as notes ascend. It's certainly possible to push and yell in an effort to delay vocal fold preferences. Once again, though—*skillful belting is more than simply shouting*. It requires precise control over vocal fold compression and resonance tuning as opposed to brute pulmonary force.

To master belting technique, we need to maintain subtle amounts of vocal fold thickness and compression while still allowing the vocal folds to be thinned and lengthened toward head voice as notes get higher. With too much breath pressure and compression, belting can quickly become shouty or strained. With too little breath pressure or compression, attempts at belting can easily crack into head voice or falsetto. If you're working on belting technique, your goal should be to master various mix voice coordinations that feature strength without force, compression without squeeze, and head resonance without head voice.

In addition, try experimenting with resonance strategies that can make your voice sound beltier. Some of these include allowing the larynx to rise, increasing the presence of twang and brighter formants, and opening the embouchure. However, when experimenting with these elements, make sure that you balance them out with nasal resonance, breath support, compression control, and volume control. If you can strike a balance that achieves the impression of power, without undesired force and volume, then you've created the conditions for your ideal and most sustainable belting. Keep in mind that the best belting is actually a lot quieter than you would ever expect!

**To sing like never before**, we must buckle up for belting and buckle down to achieve its many nuances. Chest voice and mix voice can be healthfully and sustainably brought above their customary range. However, this must be accompanied by thoughtful coordination of laryngeal muscles, breath pressure, and resonance tuning. Simple as that!

**1** Discover your belt by maintaining the qualities of your lower registers higher up in your range.

**2** As you take chest voice and mix voice higher in your range, be careful not to shout or strain.

**3** Practice belting with various volumes and resonance strategies to achieve an ideal balance.

# 60 Voice Types

## Facing the Facts, FAQs & FACHS

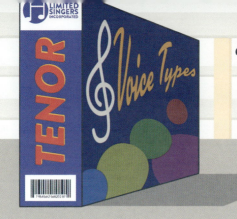

# "WHAT TYPE OF VOICE DO I HAVE?"

This is one of singing's most Frequently Asked Questions. It's a question that can, in fact, be answered. But, only if we

FACE THE FACHS!

**VOICE TYPES** (Fachs) are classifications used to identify vocal ranges and resonance characteristics. Common voice types include bass, baritone, tenor, alto, mezzo-soprano, and soprano.

The inherent *range* of a voice is primarily determined by vocal fold length and thickness. For instance, females generally have shorter and thinner vocal folds than males. Thus, females naturally have higher ranges.

The inherent *resonance characteristics* of a voice are primarily determined by the size and shape of the head, neck, mouth, larynx, pharynx, and nasal cavity. For example, larger pharynxes tend to bring out lower frequencies because the resonance tube is longer.

Vocal Fachs also categorize the manner in which a singer's vocal range is amplified by their unique resonance characteristics. While resonance is crucial to every singer's vocal technique, loud amplification (projecting) of the voice is only necessary in certain styles. For example, classical singers need to project over an orchestra, whereas contemporary singers use a microphone. As a result, Vocal Fachs apply far more to classical singing and occasionally some choral settings than they do to most contemporary styles.

While each individual has unique comfort zones or sweet spots based on their own physiology, voice typing has a much larger potential for creating limitations than it does for creating growth. With so much of singing being mental, emotional, and spiritual, most singers rightfully find it discouraging to be pigeonholed into rigid categories.

Thankfully, vocal registration is the key to unlocking the shackles of voice typing. By coordinating all of the vocal registers to their fullest potentials, a singer who might have been labelled a "low voice," can very reasonably learn to sing as a "high voice." In fact, contemporary singers can often transcend voice types to a large extent if given the proper training, practice, time, and experience.

Instead of the FAQ: "What type of voice do I have?" a contemporary singer should ask, "What type of voice do I WANT?" By coordinating vocal musculature, mastering vocal registration, and fine-tuning vocal resonance, far fewer limitations exist than most singers have historically been led to believe.

**To sing like never before**, we need to ask different questions. Rather than searching for answers to FAQs like "which Fach am I?" we should instead seek the countless ways that our voices can defy the so-called Facts!

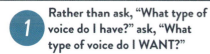 Rather than ask, "What type of voice do I have?" ask, "What type of voice do I WANT?"
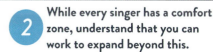 While every singer has a comfort zone, understand that you can work to expand beyond this.
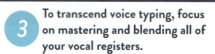 To transcend voice typing, focus on mastering and blending all of your vocal registers.

# CHAPTER 7
## LARYNX & VOCAL FOLD CONTROL

THE VOCAL FOLDS HAVE LONG BEEN VOCAL PEDAGOGY'S **BENCHWARMERS**

For generations, vocal technique has been dominated by its **"STARTING FIVE"**: BREATH SUPPORT, DROPPED JAW, RAISED SOFT PALATE, LOW LARYNX, UPRIGHT POSTURE. These singing stars have made themselves household names.

MEANWHILE, OUR PLUCKY PHONATORS WANT NOTHING MORE THAN FOR A VOCAL COACH TO GIVE THEM THEIR CHANCE TO IMPRESS. AND **COMPRESS**

**COMPRESSION** (medial compression) is the degree to which the vocal folds are brought together during phonation. As compression increases, the vocal folds become more resistant to breath exiting through them. As compression decreases, the vocal folds become more passive to the exhalation. So, compression essentially helps us add strength and solidness to our voices.

Vocal mastery is rather difficult to achieve anytime the vocal folds are left on the bench. Frankly, there are many times when all the breath, jaw, larynx, resonance, and posture work in the world can never entirely get the job done. That's why it's a game changer to learn that we can actually *control* our vocal folds!

First, let's recall which muscles are involved. The primary compression muscles are the interarytenoids, lateral cricoarytenoids, and the thyrovocalis. The lateral cricoarytenoids rotate the vocal folds together to initiate phonation and control adduction. The interarytenoids assist the vocal folds in making a clean seal at their posterior. Most valuably though, the thyrovocalis helps the vocal folds to make thicker and firmer contact from within the folds.

As chest voice ascends toward head voice, the compression muscles help the vocal folds to maintain various degrees of thickness and contact—even as they are lengthened by the cricothyroid. This allows registers like chest voice and, especially, mix voice, to not suddenly crack, break, or switch into higher registers (like head voice) sooner than we desire. This said, all registers (including higher ones) can benefit from compression because it helps ensure that we do not become weak, aspirate, or breathy.

So, how can we begin to practice and build compression in our voices? Some of the most effective tools are glottals, vocal fry, and voiced plosives.

**GLOTTALS** add compression by closing off the vocal folds completely. To discover glottals, try speaking the phrase "uh oh." Or, notice the little clicking sensation that happens at the beginning of sentences that start with a vowel, like, "I'm practicing compression," or "A glottal brings my vocal folds together."

**VOCAL FRY** encourages vocal fold contact while also reducing breath pressure. Remember the creaking sound that we explored in the vocal fry section? Try adding that sound at the beginning of a vowel (like "fry-AH" or "fry-EE") and notice how it influences the vowel.

Finally, **VOICED PLOSIVES** (B, D, and G) bring the vocal folds together while also reducing the flow of air through them. These are as easy as practicing syllables like BAY-BAY-BAY, DEE-DEE-DEE, or GOH-GOH-GOH. By emphasizing these consonants, you should instantly notice how much easier it is to stay strong, solid, and compressed. Add all three of these tools into your vocal workouts and your vocal folds will be ready to flex some muscle!

**To sing like never before**, don't throw in the towel on your vocal folds. Instead, let them play their A-game. Too often the vocal folds are asked to RIP when they are the real MVP!

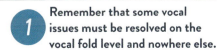 Remember that some vocal issues must be resolved on the vocal fold level and nowhere else.

 Use sounds like glottals, vocal fry, and voiced plosives to increase vocal fold compression.

 Call upon compression for smoothing out register transitions or eliminating breathiness.

Your meditation instructor begins class with a gentle affirmation and then bellows a blood-curdling -

Your librarian hands you your library book and then screams an ear-splitting -

Your lover romantically bends down on one knee and then lets out a lung-busting -

Too bad nobody taught them about

**DECOMPRESSION** is the reduction of vocal fold contact during phonation. Decompression is the direct opposite of compression, as it causes the vocal folds to come together *less* firmly and tightly. This usually makes the voice lighter, softer, and headier in quality.

When decompression is used to a large degree, the vocal folds do not make clean contact and the voice becomes aspirate. *Aspirate* refers to the presence of airiness or breathiness in a singer's tone. Aspirate qualities are a key stylistic element within most contemporary vocal styles, but they are also important for vocal technique.

Specifically, decompression and breathiness can help you lighten and loosen your voice when it's feeling too squeezed or strained. This said, be careful not to confuse breathiness with more breath. Instead, a breathy sound is simply a gentler kind of vocal fold contact that does not require increased airflow. Remember to use disciplined breath support as much with aspirate sounds as you would with any other vocal quality.

Unfortunately, singers often overemphasize compression and neglect decompression in an effort for vocal power. But, if compression gets too dominant, then the voice can become pressed, squeezed, or even raspy.

There are many strategies to solve this—lowering the larynx, maximizing resonance spaces, adjusting the breath flow, etc. Yet, the most effective and most often overlooked solution is simply asking the vocal folds to *loosen themselves* with decompression!

To experience this, try using the glottic consonant H. This is perhaps the best tool for practicing and encouraging decompression. When a gentle H initiates any vowel or vocal sound, the vocal folds begin phonation from a state of decompression. In other words, you are sort of guaranteed to get off to a good start when practicing with an H. In time, your vocal folds will learn that decompression can be controlled with tremendous nuance. Developing this kind of vocal fold control is a vital element in achieving vocal mastery.

**To sing like never before**, decompression must be valued as highly as compression. If it is, then the vocal folds will begin to possess their own independent tightening and loosening abilities. Now *that's* something to SHOUT about!

 Value decompression as highly as compression in order to achieve balance in your voice.
 Use the glottic consonant H to encourage decompression and develop vocal fold control.
 Experiment with aspirate qualities as a tool for both style and vocal technique.

Goldilocks is giving a free outdoor concert in the woods. Unfortunately, she's not very well-liked by the animals of the forest.

The bears have been especially big critics ever since Porridge-gate.

**PAPA BEAR** thinks her singing is too squeezed.

**MAMA BEAR** thinks it is too breathy.

But, **BABY BEAR** is a little more forgiving. He thinks Goldilocks' singing is "Juuuuuuust right!"

Looks like Baby Bear is a big fan of **BALANCED COMPRESSION**.

**BALANCED COMPRESSION** is the ideal equilibrium between breath flow and vocal fold compression. Too much compression causes the voice to become squeezed, pinched, or even raspy. This often suggests that the adduction muscles (lateral cricoarytenoid, interarytenoid, thyroarytenoid) are overworking. However, it can also be caused by unwanted larynx raising or tension in the jaw, tongue, and extrinsic larynx muscles. When there is too much compression, breath is less able to get past the vocal folds.

Conversely, too much decompression allows air to leak through the vocal folds. This typically indicates that the adduction muscles are too passive. It can also occur when the tongue retracts backwards or the larynx is forced into too low of a position.

In between compression and decompression is balanced compression. It is neither too pressed nor too breathy. Instead, it results in crisp, clear, and clean singing. Balanced compression should be every singer's neutral setting in terms of optimal technique and vocal health.

This is not to say that balanced compression is the only good way to sing. When used as a conscious stylistic choice, overly compressed or decompressed sounds can be highly desirable. Rock singers, for example, frequently use edgier, grittier, and tighter sounds. Pop, R&B, and jazz singers often use lighter, softer, and breathier sounds. In most styles, we want to be able to move freely between many different vocal textures (breathy, clean, compressed, etc.). However, it's important to prioritize our balanced sounds before departing into more dramatically compressed or decompressed sounds. This will ensure that our voices do not become either too heavy or too light.

One of the best ways to practice balanced compression is to exercise with trills and fricatives. *Trills* are phonemes that vibrate the tongue or the lips. *Fricatives* are consonants that create friction as the breath passes through the tongue or lips. *Unvoiced fricatives* (S, F, voiceless TH, and SH) do not use the vocal folds to make sound, whereas *voiced fricatives* (Z, V, voiced TH, and ZH) do use the vocal folds. All trills and voiced fricatives help to achieve balanced compression by requiring sounds to be made through a constant and even airstream. Practice trills and voiced fricatives to discover balanced compression regardless of your vocal style!

**To sing like never before**, get a good night's sleep in someone else's cozy bed so that you can start your day on a high note! However, when you warm up the next morning, just remember that your first goal is to achieve balance. Not too loose. Not too tight. Juuuust right!

 Ask yourself if your compression feels too tight, too loose, or "JUUUUST right."

 Regardless of style, balanced compression is the neutral setting for optimal vocal technique.

 Practice exercises or songs with trills or voiced fricatives to achieve balanced compression.

# 64 Neutral Larynx Position

You've got a major job interview coming up. So, naturally you're growing nervous. Friends and family try to be supportive. They encourage you to "Just Be Yourself!"

But, you're a singer. So, you know that's easier said than done.

You understand that to truly be yourself, you'll have to maintain a
**NEUTRAL LARYNX POSITION!**

The **NEUTRAL LARYNX POSITION** is the position of the larynx when it is at rest. In both singing and speaking, it's also the larynx's relative location when it is not being moved for technical or stylistic reasons. A good rule of thumb is this: the neutral larynx position should sound the most like YOU.

In general, larynx movement during singing is necessary and beneficial. For example, contemporary singers often employ high larynx positions for their brighter and lighter qualities. Meanwhile, classical singers frequently use low larynx positions for their darker and richer qualities. However, the neutral position is foundational in *all* styles because it helps us to achieve our most authentic (or least stylized) sounds.

The neutral larynx position can also be considered our default setting in terms of vocal technique, health, and freedom. While we've seen that it is necessary for the larynx to be a style changer, optimal technique requires that we minimize its tendency to be a pitch changer.

This tendency to raise our larynx for pitch is hardwired into us from an early age. As infants, we cry out anytime we want something. Our volume increases, our pitch rises, our mouths open, and you guessed it: our larynx goes up! Thus, it learns to rise radically as pitches ascend, and drop drastically as pitches descend. While this is perfectly normal in life, severe larynx movement with respect to pitch is one of the worst habits in singing. It denies the vocal folds their job as pitch changers, and can even lead to fatigue, strain, and overwork.

Perhaps the best way to discover the neutral larynx position is simply to feel it. By placing two fingers gently on your larynx, you can easily monitor its position. (Remember to never hold it in a fixed place.) Try swallowing to feel its extreme high position and try yawning to feel its extreme low position. Then, relax to feel it rest right in the middle.

As you sing, you will notice your larynx moving somewhat as pitches move up and down. Again, this is perfectly natural. However, absolutely transformative results will happen if you can keep this movement to a minimum. As you practice, you'll start developing quite a bit of awareness and control over your larynx's behavior just by monitoring it with gentle physical touch.

**To sing like never before**, the neutral larynx position should be the first thing listed on your vocal resume. If it is, then you're hired! The job should be a breeze. Because when your larynx is neutral… your voice does no unnecessary hard labor!

 **1** While the larynx should move somewhat with respect to pitch, strive to minimize this tendency. **2** Place your fingers gently on your larynx to monitor its movement as pitches rise and fall. **3** If it rises drastically as pitches rise, try practicing with a lower and "yawnier" larynx.

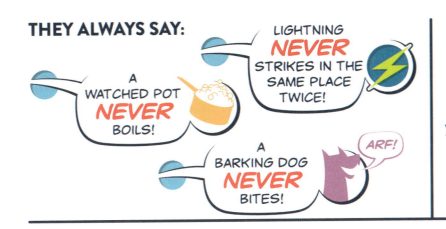 

**HIGH LARYNX POSITIONS** occur when the larynx lifts above its neutral position. Many singers have been taught (often fearfully) that they should *never* lift the larynx. Yet, there are actually several stylistic and technical situations in which it is appropriate and necessary to do so.

For example, high larynx positions are foundational features of most contemporary styles like rock, pop, R&B, musical theatre, and jazz. So, while we want to discourage the larynx from being too much of a pitch changer, we can still encourage it to be a style changer. A good rule of thumb is:

*Raise your larynx as a stylistic choice. Don't raise it as a technical necessity.*

This said, high larynx positions do offer several technical advantages. First, they provide brighter and more youthful sounds by shortening the pharynx and boosting brighter resonances (raising all formants). Next, vocal fold compression increases naturally whenever the larynx is raised. In the right circumstances this can help keep the voice more solid without having to work as hard with compression muscles or breath pressure. Finally, higher larynx positions facilitate softer volumes, making the voice more suited for microphone singing.

With all of these benefits, why do people sometimes say to never raise the larynx? Well, these positions are feared by some because they can indeed be unhealthy and even injurious to the voice under certain conditions. The most important health consideration is to know that high larynx positions are *not* conducive to loud volumes.

You see, whenever there is a high degree of *both* vocal fold contact and breath pressure, significant stress is placed on the vocal folds. The increased compression caused by a raised larynx combined with loud volumes and breath pressure create a perfect storm for vocal health. So, make sure you don't try to project your voice loudly when singing with a high larynx position. Instead, emphasize skills like decompression, breath support, and nasal resonance. If you do, then raising your larynx can be as healthy and sustainable as any other vocal coordination.

**To sing like never before,** high larynx positions are better late than never. If executed with wisdom, they are as safe as eating leftovers next to a sleeping dog on a sunny day!

**1** Don't fear high larynx positions. Instead, use them wisely for appropriate styles and skills.

**2** High larynx positions can facilitate brighter tone, greater compression, and softer volumes.

**3** Make sure that your high larynx positions are never accompanied by loud or forceful volume.

| | | | | |
|---|---|---|---|---|
| "INCREASES TO PHARYNGEAL SIZE HAVE A CORRESPONDING RELATIONSHIP WITH THE LOWERING OF FORMANT FREQUENCIES." | BLANK STARE | "THE FUNCTIONALITY OF THE CRICOTHYROID JOINT IS ENHANCED PROPORTIONALLY WITH RESPECT TO LARYNGEAL DEPTH." | GLANCES AT WRISTWATCH | "THE POSSIBILITY OF AN INVERSE CORRELATION BETWEEN STERNOHYOID ACTIVITY AND GLOTTAL RESISTANCE IS A FASCINATING HYPOTHESIS." |

YAWN

Well, you may be bored. But, at least you've discovered your **LOW LARYNX POSITION!**

**LOW LARYNX POSITIONS** occur when the larynx drops below its neutral position. In life, our larynxes lower unconsciously every time we yawn. In singing, our larynxes lower as a conscious means of lengthening the pharynx. This increased pharyngeal size accommodates a variety of technical and stylistic abilities.

For several generations, it was common for singers to be taught to sing exclusively with low larynx positions. This was because a lowered larynx was thought to be superior in terms of health and function. The origins of this belief stemmed largely from the fact that these positions are found in many classical and traditional styles. These styles do indeed benefit from lowering the larynx in order to safely accommodate louder sounds that are projected without the assistance of any electronic amplification.

In contemporary vocal pedagogy, it is understood that all larynx positions can be healthy and useful—especially with the use of the microphone for amplification. Nevertheless, regardless of vocal style, low larynx positions will always remain an essential tool for every singer in terms of volume, resonance, and technique.

## VOLUME

Low larynx positions help with volume in several ways. They create a larger pharyngeal space, which increases our resonance potential. They also cause the vocal folds to have less inherent tension. This provides an advantageous starting point for adding compression (glottal resistance). Finally, low larynx positions help air to flow more freely through the larynx.

If you've never felt how this works, try a yawn and notice all three elements: your throat opens, your vocal folds loosen, and air can flow quite freely in and out. Once you've felt this setup, you've discovered the ideal conditions for adding some volume to your voice. Resonance space, controlled glottal resistance, and airflow are the quintessential elements of volume and dynamics.

## RESONANCE

Low larynx positions add darker vocal resonances (lower formants) to the voice. Excessive brightness (frequently mistaken for nasality) is a common concern for singers. If your voice is consistently brighter than you would like it to be, then there is perhaps no better solution than lowering your larynx. Even if you won't ultimately sing with a low larynx position, it is important to explore the darkest qualities in your voice. After you've felt the extremes, it is much easier to find a balance. Balancing bright and dark resonances has historically been called "chiaroscuro." *Chiaroscuro* is an Italian word which aptly means "bright dark." Explore lowering your larynx to help you achieve your ideal resonance balance.

## TECHNIQUE

Finally, low larynx positions are essential for overall technique. They are the best method for combating the larynx's habit of being a pitch changer. Remember that most singers struggle with raising the larynx too much as pitches ascend. If that's the case for you, try lowering your larynx as you move through your vocal range. Again, this isn't intended to be your final product, since you'll probably sound too dark while practicing this. However, by exaggerating a low larynx position as an exercise, your larynx will learn to break the habit of automatically moving upwards as pitches go up. From here, you'll experience a great deal more control and ease—regardless of your vocal style.

**To sing like never before**, you don't have to pretend that vocal pedagogy isn't boring sometimes. You don't even have to suppress that yawn. Why not go with it instead? After all—what goes up, must come down!

  **1** Try crescendoing with a lowered larynx. Observe how it accommodates louder volumes.  **2** If your larynx always rises for high notes, practice lowering it a little as pitches rise.  **3** If your vocal tone is often too bright, experiment with low larynx positions as a solution.

Once upon a time, there lived Snow White. She was the purest and loveliest lass in the land. But, don't let her demure demeanor fool you. This chick ROCKS! If you think she's waiting around for some sloth, hero, or dragon... thou art mistaken! This princess hangs with the ultimate rock band -

## The Seven Dwarfs of Distortion!

**SCRATCHY, BREATHY, FRY, UNTRUTHFUL, SQUEEZY, GROWLY, and VELUMPY!**

**DISTORTION** refers to raspy vocal sounds that are sometimes used as stylistic effects. These effects often convey edginess, grit, or emotion to serve as a contrast to cleaner vocal productions.

Distortion techniques can pose some serious vocal health risks if performed improperly. So, most singers would be wise to steer clear of this thicket of thorns altogether—especially if your style does not need these aesthetics. On the other hand, many contemporary singers perform these effects consistently while still maintaining health and longevity. As we will see, staying healthy requires us to make sure that the true vocal folds aren't compromised while various distortions are performed. So, can our princess ROCK and still keep her vocal folds snowy white? If she can, then we can. Let's meet the dwarfs!

### SCRATCHY—THE DWARF OF DYSPHONIA

*Dysphonia* includes dramatic vocal injuries such as nodules, polyps, cysts, hemorrhages, and several others. However, it can also manifest itself as more benign sorts of wear and tear. Most damage occurs within the superficial lamina propria and at the epithelium. When these layers are compromised in any way, vocal fold closure is altered and various degrees of distortion can result. If you have any concerns about your voice or dysphonia, consult a trusted laryngologist or ENT doctor.

Hopefully, no singer would ever seek to harm their own voice! Nevertheless, some singers have made successful careers capitalizing on the unique qualities resulting from the character that has formed in their voices over time. As long as they don't create any further harm, vocal idiosyncrasies of this nature can actually be among the healthiest varieties of distortion. In other words, singers with dysphonic qualities that stem from harmless preexisting conditions actually don't need to manipulate their voices at all to create distortion elements. If this is you, stay encouraged. There is plenty of room in the world of singing for imperfect voices. But, again, please never seek out this kind of damage.

### BREATHY—THE DWARF OF DECOMPRESSION

As we've seen, breathiness is created by decompressing the vocal folds to create aspirate or airy sounds. All contemporary styles use breathiness to convey intimacy, emotion, and texture. At times, though, it can be considered a distortion feature due to the noise elements that it creates.

While breathiness can certainly be used by itself, it is also quite effective when combined with other distortion varieties. Specifically, it provides vocal fold decompression while constriction for other distortions is being added elsewhere. You see, most distortion varieties risk over-compressing the vocal folds. Yet, breathiness can help reduce this compression. For this reason, it is among the most important skills to cultivate before exploring the other kinds of distortion. By developing your aspirate sounds first, you create the potential for more aggressive-sounding distortions to be performed more efficiently later.

**To sing like never before**, we must meet all seven dwarfs. So, this fairy tale is... to be continued...

> **Disclaimer:** Always exercise caution when experimenting with all distortion varieties. Pain and hoarseness are not okay. Study with a distortion specialist for mastery of the skills introduced in this section.

---

**SLNB QUICK TIPS**

**1** Distortion isn't for everybody, but it can indeed be sustainable within the styles that require it.

**2** NEVER seek to hurt your voice! Yet, know there is room in the world for "imperfect" voices.

**3** Practice breathy qualities as a first step before exploring other distortion varieties.

*Let's not delay this vocal fairy tale for even a moment!*

*"Heigh Ho! Heigh Ho! It's off to Rasp we go…"*

## FRY—THE DWARF OF VOCAL FRY DISTORTION

As we've seen, vocal fry is its own vocal register beneath the chest voice. However, fry qualities can also be maintained on notes far higher than vocal fry's native range in order to produce vocal fry distortion. To experience this, try moving gently back and forth between a light vocal fry and a very softly sung pitch. With some practice, you'll notice that fry qualities can exist simultaneously with several pitches throughout your range.

Vocal fry distortion has some health considerations from the standpoint that it is produced directly at the vocal fold level. Thankfully, it's quite difficult to achieve this distortion while pushing harmful amounts of breath and volume. Gentle airflow is actually one of the keys to success with it. Additionally, resonance tuning and the use of a microphone are ultimately what create its power. These factors allow many singers to perform vocal fry distortion safely.

## UNTRUTHFUL—THE DWARF OF FALSE VOCAL FOLD DISTORTION

The false vocal folds constrict during everyday gestures like hacking or whispering. However, when the false vocal folds are brought together skillfully and with nuance, they can be used to produce distortion. False vocal fold distortion is arguably the most popular and common variety of distortion among contemporary singers.

This distortion is easiest to find when using gestures that constrict the larynx and pharynx, such as twang. Try whispering or speaking a very bright and brassy "YEAH!" This creates a subtle, yet noticeable constriction. This kind of light constriction encourages the false vocal folds to make contact and produce distortion.

Due to their cruder design and function, impact to the false vocal folds is not a health concern like it is with the true vocal folds. Nevertheless, their close proximity to one another is important to consider. When using false vocal fold distortion, we must ensure that the true vocal folds do not also become overly compressed. By learning to consciously regulate vocal fold compression, the false vocal folds can constrict *above* to create distortion without compromising the true vocal folds *below*.

## SQUEEZY—THE DWARF OF ARYTENOID DISTORTION

Arytenoid distortion occurs when the arytenoid cartilages are squeezed together to create a vibration. It is almost never subtle. In speech, this distortion is used quite frequently to imitate the stereotypical sound of an evil or monstrous character. In singing, it's usually reserved for extremely distorted moments within many musical styles, but it appears most frequently in styles like hard rock/metal, gospel, and throat singing.

Arytenoid distortion can be discovered most easily by humming and then performing a gentle throat clear. Pretty quickly, a sort of rolling or rattling begins to happen. From there, opening the mouth into any vowel reveals the full effect of the distortion.

Like all distortion varieties, it is possible to perform arytenoid distortion safely and sustainably. However, due to the considerable constriction inside the larynx, it's important to make sure that it is not done too aggressively or performed with excessive breath pressure. Use disciplined breath support and take care to not squeeze too violently when experimenting with arytenoid distortion.

**To sing like never before**, you don't have to whistle while you work. But, you do have to meet two more dwarfs…

**Disclaimer:** Always exercise caution when experimenting with all distortion varieties. Pain and hoarseness are not okay. Study with a distortion specialist for mastery of the skills introduced in this section.

1. Vocal fry distortion can be found by lightly dragging vocal fry qualities to higher pitches.

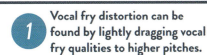

2. False fold distortion can be encouraged by subtly constricting, as in a whisper or a hack.

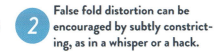

3. Arytenoid distortion can be discovered by performing a gentle throat clear through a hum.

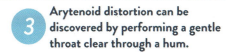

# "Mirror, mirror, on the wall – who's the RASPIEST of them all?"

Let's meet the last two Dwarfs...

## GROWLY—THE DWARF OF EPIGLOTTIC DISTORTION

Epiglottic distortion is also called "growl." It is produced by the arytenoids vibrating against the epiglottis. However, this can only happen if the epiglottis has been brought towards the back of the larynx with the tongue's base. Jazz legend Louis Armstrong is perhaps the most famous for epiglottic distortion, but the Cookie Monster is a close second. Growling is used occasionally in most contemporary styles as a textural effect.

The easiest way to discover epiglottic distortion is by tensing the tongue's base (with the hyoglossus). From here, a gentle throat clear usually invokes epiglottic distortion by setting the arytenoids into vibration against the epiglottis.

Despite its gruff and gravelly aesthetic, epiglottic distortion can be produced safely, since it takes place a considerable distance from the vocal folds. Nevertheless, breath support and compression control are important considerations for performing growls healthfully.

## VELUMPY—THE DWARF OF VELAR DISTORTION

*Velum* is the anatomical term for the soft palate. Velar distortion occurs when the soft palate and tongue base vibrate against each other. This is easily experienced by imitating a tiger or performing uvular consonants commonly found in languages like Hebrew and French. When extended for several seconds, velar distortion produces a snarling or aggressive hissing quality.

Velar distortion is not used frequently, but some distortion-dominant styles add it as a complementary feature to other distortion elements. Although it has a fierce quality, it is the only distortion that doesn't impact the larynx directly. This makes it quite safe and sustainable to use when needed.

The moral of the story: distortion doesn't have to poison your Adam's apple. Nevertheless, our fairest female must be conscientious if she wants her cords to stay pure as snow while rocking out with these madcap miners.

Above all, performing distortion sustainably requires shrewd awareness of breath support. The additional compression and constriction of the larynx necessary for most distortion varieties must also be executed with subtlety and precision. Experienced distortion performers rely on the microphone as much as possible. They also seek strategies to reduce any burden on the true vocal folds as additional burdens are placed upon other areas in the throat.

**To sing like never before**, you don't need to perform distortion unless your style absolutely requires it. However, if it does, then don't let fear dwarf your ability to perform distortion responsibly. Your vocal folds can still live happily ever after!

**Disclaimer:** Always exercise caution when experimenting with all distortion varieties. Pain and hoarseness are not okay. Study with a distortion specialist for mastery of the skills introduced in this section.

  Epiglottic distortion can be felt by tensing the tongue's base and performing a gentle throat clear.  Velar distortions can be discovered by vibrating the tongue against the soft palate with a snarl.  Most distortions have risks, but can be sustainable with breath support, precision, and wisdom.

| + HE LIKES LONG WALKS ON THE BEACH. | SHE LIKES SHORT SPRINTS IN THE MOUNTAINS. − |
| --- | --- |
| + HE'S A SKILLED CONVERSATIONALIST. | SHE'S A SKILLED AERIALIST. − |
| + HE WANTS A PARTNER TO "COMPLETE." | SHE WANTS A PARTNER TO COMPETE. − |

Okay... so maybe they are a bit of an odd couple. Nevertheless, these two are as inseparable as...

# STRAIGHT TONE & VIBRATO!

**STRAIGHT TONE** is produced when notes are sung precisely and with minimal to no pitch oscillation. **VIBRATO** is produced by oscillating a sung note slightly above and below its intended pitch. Vibrato takes place primarily on the vocal fold level via the interaction between the larynx's pitch-changing muscles (thyroarytenoid and cricothyroid). However, it can also be produced by laryngeal movement or by alterations in breath pressure.

When using vibrato, your pitch variance should rarely be wide enough to disrupt the clarity of the intended note, but should instead complement it with a sort of stylistic shimmer. Most acceptable vibrato speeds oscillate around 5-7 Hz (5-7 oscillations per second). Faster speeds are sometimes called "tremolo," whereas slower speeds are sometimes called a "wobble."

Straight tone and vibrato occur together in virtually every musical style. Some styles, like opera, use vibrato more dominantly while other styles, like pop and jazz, use straight tone more often. It's exceedingly uncommon for vocal styles to use either skill exclusively. In most cases, they complement one another and balance each other out to serve the needs of each style. In other words, straight tone can be used when vibrato is inappropriate stylistically and vice versa. In some instances, it's even appropriate to begin a held note with straight tone and end it with vibrato.

Vibrato can be learned through vocal exercises involving agility, repeated staccato onsets, and register blending. Try agility exercises (fast moving exercises) to train the vocal folds to change pitch quickly. Practice repeated staccato onset exercises (like HAH-HAH-HAH) to stimulate vibrato by rapidly articulating the vocal folds.

Most importantly, use registration blending exercises to help you move throughout your entire vocal range in a smooth and even way. Balanced vocal registration, perhaps more than anything else, is the key to finding a vibrato that is consistent and effortless.

While the majority of singers strive to develop vibrato, there are some who struggle to unlearn it. Singers who have been trained to use vibrato on every note often find it difficult to rediscover their straight tone. If that's you, try singing notes in a simple, plain, and speech-like fashion. At first, this will probably sound like a bland or boring way to sing. However, once you regain the steadiness of your straight tone, you will cherish having the control to go back and forth between the two anytime you'd like.

**To sing like never before**, opposites must attract. That means that vibrato and straight tone need to work together in our voices as equals. Ultimately, vocal mastery requires us to consciously move between them at our liberty. So, may their differences forever complement one another... as they vibrate—straight into the sunset...

---

**SLNB QUICK TIPS**

**1** Practice agility, repeated staccato onsets, and register blending exercises to develop vibrato.

**2** Try singing notes as plainly, simply, and conversationally as possible to achieve straight tone.

**3** For vocal mastery, develop the ability to use vibrato or straight tone as a conscious choice.

# CHAPTER 8
*VOCAL HEALTH & SPEECH*

## 71 Hydration — SHOW 'EM WHAT YOU'RE MADE OF!

If waves ever greeted your ankles while you gazed reverently at twilight's horizon... If a random rainstorm was ever your skin's sweet salvation from a summer-scorched day... If your throbbing bones ever begged to be buried beneath bubble bath foam... ...then you know a thing or two about water.

But, here's something you might not know: **MORE THAN HALF OF YOUR BODY IS WATER.**

**THAT'S RIGHT!** More of you is **WATER** than it is **ANY OTHER THING!**

**HYDRATION** is the process of supplying sufficient amounts of water to the body. Hydration boasts boundless benefits including skin appearance, energy levels, physical fitness, and overall health.

The most obvious consideration for achieving optimal hydration is *quantity*. For most people, this amounts to roughly two liters of water per day. For singers, though, it's not only important to consider hydration simply in terms of quantity. It's even more important to consider hydration in terms of timing.

Drinking water intermittently while singing might feel nice, but it's actually too late to impact overall hydration. When we swallow, liquids don't come into contact with the vocal folds. Instead, they are pushed into the esophagus. So, if we want the vocal folds to be hydrated, then water must be consumed far enough in advance to make a difference. It's best to drink water at least 1-2 hours before singing. This allows ample time for liquids to move through the body and for the hydration process to be completed.

Both the interior and exterior of the vocal folds rely on hydration for optimal function. The exterior is coated in watery mucus that is very similar to the saliva inside your mouth. This mucus helps protect the vocal folds from fatigue and injury. Likewise, the interior layers of the vocal folds move more quickly, easily, and efficiently when hydrated. Singers that commit to a daily hydration routine are invariably surprised and pleased at the significant vocal improvements that result from a change as elementary as H2O.

**To sing like never before**, we don't need to drink water merely as a rote discipline. Instead, we need to appreciate it because it's what we actually are! At the staggering sight of the ocean, we feel gratitude. At the familiar fall of rain, we feel peace. At the serene soaking of a bath, we feel bliss. This is not a coincidence. It's our aquatic roots rejoicing in recognition of what we're made of. There's never been a better reason to hydrate!

**SLNB QUICK TIPS**

1. Don't forget that your vocal folds rely on hydration for optimal function.
2. Create a daily hydration plan for yourself that feels manageable and sustainable.
3. Keep in mind that the timing of your hydration matters as much as the quantity.

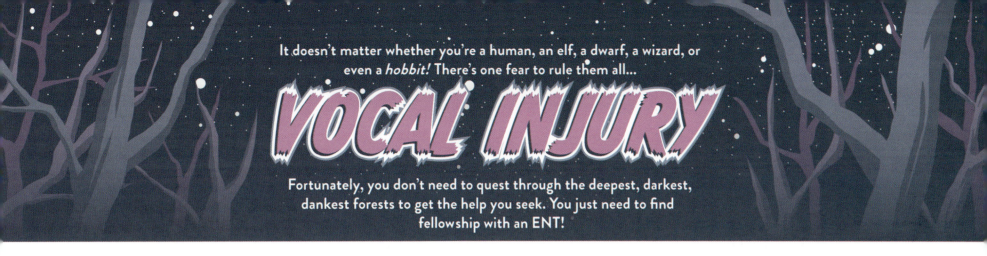

It doesn't matter whether you're a human, an elf, a dwarf, a wizard, or even a *hobbit!* There's one fear to rule them all...

# VOCAL INJURY

Fortunately, you don't need to quest through the deepest, darkest, dankest forests to get the help you seek. You just need to find fellowship with an ENT!

An **ENT** (ear, nose, and throat doctor) is a medical professional trained to diagnose and treat problems related to the ear canal, nasal cavity, pharynx, larynx, and vocal folds. It's immensely beneficial for singers of all levels to establish a relationship with a trusted ENT. Although ENTs are ordinarily qualified in many facets of health care, don't be hasty! It's wise to take your time to find an ENT who specializes in the singing voice.

The most important examination an ENT performs is called a laryngoscopy. A *laryngoscopy* is a procedure used to examine the vocal folds. It is conducted by inserting a specialized camera through the mouth or nose. Images and videos captured allow ENTs to diagnose whether the vocal folds suffer from any kind of injury, pathology, or abnormality.

Vocal injuries are varied and wide-ranging. The most noteworthy examples include nodes, cysts, polyps, and hemorrhages. While the thought of any vocal injury is traumatizing to most singers, the good news is that virtually all of them are treatable. In the vast majority of cases, complete recovery is possible with attention, care, and treatment from a qualified ENT.

Unfortunately, it's common for singers to resist seeing an ENT until there is a serious problem. Singers should instead seek to establish a relationship with one when all is going well with their singing and vocal health. ENTs can perform a baseline laryngoscopy to view the vocal folds when they are healthy. If something happens to go wrong in the future, then previous data helps to inform an accurate diagnosis and solve potential problems more quickly. (As an added incentive for an ENT visit—it's a thrilling experience to see your own vocal folds for the first time!)

**To sing like never before**, we mustn't lose the forest for the trees. Vocal injuries can certainly be terrifying. But, a new day will come. Just when everything appears darkest for our vocal health, the sun will "shine out the clearer." All thanks to the ENTs who can bravely lead us out of the woods!

**1** Establish a relationship with an ENT in your community who specializes in the singing voice.

**2** Have a laryngoscopy done when you are healthy so that you know what "normal" looks like.

**3** Never panic! Remember that almost all vocal injuries can be treated successfully.

# 73 The Singer's Diet

### Have Your Herbal Tea & Drink It Too

The **SINGER'S DIET** is any nutritional regimen specifically intended to enhance vocal function. Countless singers are bound by fear, shame, and hearsay when it comes to what they are "supposed" to eat and drink. Yet, truthfully, dietary needs are as unique to each person as the singing voice itself. That's why the most important aspect of the singer's diet is to not view foods judgmentally, but categorically.

## REFLUX

*Acid reflux* is a condition in which digestive acids irritate the esophagus, larynx, and sometimes even the vocal folds themselves. Common culprits include spicy or fatty foods, citrus, caffeine, and alcohol. The vast majority of people do not suffer from acid reflux severe enough to cause problems. However, some cases of acid reflux can be quite detrimental to vocal health. In those instances, an ENT might suggest dietary and lifestyle adjustments or prescribe temporary corrective medications. If you notice a certain food or beverage causing acid reflux or vocal problems, start by eliminating it for a while to see if that helps. You can always add it back in moderation once you've identified what you are sensitive to.

## ENERGY

Voice practice sessions and lessons are essentially rehearsals for performance. So, use them to rehearse your diet. Experiment with which proteins, carbohydrates, fruits, and vegetables generate energy and make your voice feel the best.

## HYDRATION

Liquids are not necessarily hydrating just because they're liquids. Beverages high in caffeine, alcohol, and sugar can actually have a dehydrating effect. Aside from your daily water intake, observe which liquids your voice tolerates well and keep you feeling hydrated.

## TEMPERATURE

Singers commonly fear that hot or cold beverages will harm their voices. Fortunately, liquids don't come near enough to the vocal folds to significantly affect them. This said, some singers are more sensitive to temperature than others. Monitor whether certain temperatures feel soothing, quenching, or compromising to your instrument.

## TIMING

Many singers like to have a small meal before singing. Others swear by singing on an empty stomach. Experiment with both the quantity and the timing of meals to achieve your ideal equilibrium.

**To sing like never before**, consider how deeply, how closely, and how lovingly you want your audience to listen to you. Then, consider listening to your body in the same way. Tuning in to your voice's specific requirements allows you to have your cake and eat it too. Just as long as you save the icing for your audience!

---

  Create a singer's diet for yourself that is not based on fear, but on your body's unique needs.  Experiment with various foods to see how they affect acid reflux, energy, and hydration.  Learn to listen to your body to determine the right variety, quantity, and timing of your meals.

 **Smoking & Alcohol**

**SMOKING AND ALCOHOL** are habits that can negatively affect vocal health. While both are potentially deleterious, there's a sizable disparity between smoking and alcohol in terms of their consequences.

Smoking, aside from being deadly, is among the most disastrous decisions that a singer could make for their vocal health. Smoking involves breathing toxic chemicals directly across the larynx, vocal folds, trachea, and lungs. This causes irritation, inflammation, and even injury to the vocal folds. It also severely inhibits lung function. For singers, this impairment of both the vocal folds and lungs jeopardizes breath control, stamina, registration, range, and ease of production. So, it's safe to say that smoking harms the voice. Period. Any serious or aspiring singer should seek to quit smoking as immediately as possible.

Alcohol, on the other hand, is the clear vice of choice for the singing voice. Unlike smoke, alcohol doesn't touch the vocal folds or lungs. When we swallow, the larynx and epiglottis push liquids into the esophagus instead of the trachea. Liquids bypass the larynx, vocal folds, and lungs entirely. While excessive alcohol consumption is highly destructive, small and moderate consumption causes virtually no harm in most instances. Nevertheless, there are still a few health considerations when it comes to alcohol.

First, alcohol is usually consumed in loud bars, clubs, and social settings. Talking loudly over clamorous crowds is colossally more compromising than any one alcoholic beverage could ever be. So, it's important to be mindful of environmental hazards when drinking.

Next, alcohol can contribute to acid reflux for some singers. In these cases, alcohol can have a larger impact on the voice because of the inflammation caused by reflux. Singers with acid reflux problems may need to avoid alcohol completely or use it more cautiously than other singers.

Lastly, alcohol affects hydration. Drinking plenty of water any time you drink alcohol helps to minimize its dehydrating effects. Water consumption also helps to ensure that alcoholic beverages are consumed in moderation.

**To sing like never before**, we must smoke like... never ever. And we must drink like... never excessively. It's easy to ask yourself whether smoking and alcohol are harming your singing. It's hard to ask yourself "What could have been?"

  **Quitting smoking is one of the best things that you can do for your vocal health.**  **If you drink alcohol, then partaking wisely and in moderation typically causes little or no harm.**  **Remember that loud social settings are often more of a culprit than moderate drinking.**

**LISTEN UP!** It's about time that our **PHYSIQUE** matched our **TECHNIQUE**. And you know what that means, don't you? **LESS LIP TRILLS** MORE TREADMILLS! **LESS CORD COMPRESSION** MORE BENCH PRESSIN'! **LESS DIAPHRAGM** MORE DIET PLAN! The only way our **PERSPIRATION** can ever rival our **INSPIRATION** is with **VOCAL FITNESS**.

**VOCAL FITNESS** means conditioning the physical body in ways that complement vocal technique. Physical fitness is beneficial to all people. However, vocal fitness requires singers to weigh a few ups and downs.

## THE UPs

### POSTURE
Adding weight training and stretching to your vocal fitness routine can positively impact your posture and alignment. Weight training helps balance and tone overall musculature. Daily stretching helps alleviate tension and facilitates freedom of movement. Yoga is also particularly advantageous for blending strength and flexibility while simultaneously improving breath management.

### BREATHING
To enhance your lung health and breath efficiency, try adding cardiovascular exercise to your vocal fitness. All singers will notice improvements in their breathing after undertaking a consistent cardiovascular activity. It's also wise for singers who dance or move a lot onstage to experiment with some cardiovascular movement within vocal practice sessions to simulate onstage conditions.

### ENDURANCE
As you sustain a consistent vocal fitness routine, you should notice an improvement to your practice and performance energy. The consistent combination of strength training, cardiovascular exercise, yoga, and stretching promote both physical and vocal endurance.

## THE DOWNs

### ABDOMINAL OVERDEVELOPMENT
Abdominal fitness and core strength are fundamental for all athletes. However, overdeveloping the core can compromise the vocal breathing system by restricting movement in the abdominal area. Thus, core exercises should be counterbalanced with stretches like upward-facing dog, cobra pose, and backbends. This ensures that toned abdominals still remain pliable.

### NECK STRAIN
Some core and upper body exercises (i.e. crunches and shrugs) tend to strain the neck muscles. This strain in the neck places undue pressure on the larynx and vocal folds. Be mindful of your neck while exercising. It's wise to modify any athletic movements that frequently cause neck strain.

### VALSALVA MANEUVER
Although the Valsalva maneuver is one of the body's natural mechanisms for lifting heavy objects, misusing Valsalva is ruinous to the voice. When highly pressurized air is thrust against closed vocal folds (like during a heaving or grunting sound), it can be extremely taxing or even injurious. Singers who participate in intense weight training must be mindful to exhale through fricative consonants (like S or SH) instead of pushing against closed folds.

**To sing like never before**, physical activity should work for your voice and not against it. So, go ahead and put the THIGH back in thyroarytenoid. Just be careful to not put the CRY back in cricothyroid!

---

  Establish a physical fitness routine that best complements your vocal technique.  Combine strength training, cardio, and stretching to benefit both your health and your singing.  Modify any workouts that cause abdominal overdevelopment, neck strain, or vocal fold fatigue.

## 76 Developing a Practice Plan

### YOU MUST TAKE THE… "N TRAIN"?

A **PRACTICE PLAN** is a disciplined vocal regimen designed to maximize growth and excellence. Just like mastering any musical instrument, vocal mastery can only come from years of practice. Ideal practice plans vary from singer to singer. So, it's important to find the plan that works best for you.

If possible, develop your practice plan with a trusted voice teacher who can make suggestions for your improvement and recommend appropriate vocal exercises. *Vocal exercises* (vocalises) are vocal patterns designed to build vocal technique in specific ways during practice. All practice plans should reflect three core qualities: balance, focus, and consistency.

## BALANCE
Practice plans should include both vocal exercises and song work. Practicing vocal exercises exclusively may result in technical proficiency, but also a lack of style, soul, and expressiveness. On the other hand, practicing songs exclusively is enjoyable, but may result in a lack of vocal awareness, precision, and specificity. Make sure that your practice plan strikes the ideal balance for your growth.

## FOCUS
Practice sessions should aim to address specific vocal issues. It's okay to sing just for fun on occasion. However, best results are achieved when there is an intentional focus. For example, vocal exercises should never be thought of merely as warmups. Instead, they should be regarded as the most direct method for targeting and correcting specific vocal limitations.

## CONSISTENCY
It's better to practice more often than to practice for excessively long (and potentially fatiguing) durations. Five to six days per week for 20-90 minutes is usually an ideal scenario. While some singers might benefit from longer practice sessions, most will experience optimal growth when practice sessions become a sustainable part of daily life.

**To sing like never before**, you could take the N train to get to Carnegie Hall, but practice will always be the better route. With a proper practice plan, you'll never need to ask anyone how to get where you want to be. You'll already be headed in the right direction—towards the kind of success that can only be achieved by hard work!

  Establish a practice plan that strikes a balance between vocal exercises and song work.  Focus your practice plan on correcting and improving specific areas of vocal technique.  Make sure that your practice plan is achievable so that it can be sustainable and consistent.

## 77 Vocal Rest — A Rested Development

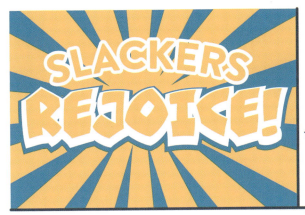      

**VOCAL REST** is any conservation strategy intended to heal, protect, or restore the voice. Work ethic is certainly essential to vocal success. Yet, most singers are surprised to find that transformative results can arise from vocal rest as much as they can from hard work. Here are some aspects of vocal rest that can make a big difference:

### SLEEP

Sleep is the body's natural mechanism for restoring our minds and muscles. Singing might not be the same as doing calculus or bench pressing, but it's still a mental and muscular task. Sleep is imperative for ensuring that your voice's fine-tuned and intricate muscle coordinations become skillful, repeatable, and consistent. A good night's rest is particularly important after a successful practice, lesson, rehearsal, or performance. Proper sleep helps your breakthroughs to become your norm.

### MARKING

*Marking* means singing a song or passage more lightly or softly in rehearsal than it would normally be sung in a performance. Marking allows a singer to not give everything before a big performance, and to save it for the stage instead.

### SINGING SABBATH

Just as workouts shouldn't be done seven days per week, the same thing is true for vocal practice. Highly-focused singers are sometimes hesitant to take a day off for fear of losing progress. However, the opposite tends to be the case. That is, taking a singing sabbath each week typically yields far greater results in terms of improvement, health, and longevity.

### LONGER REST PERIODS

Vocal muscles are usually more coordination-based than strength-based. As a result, dramatic changes to the singing voice typically take a long time to attain. Thankfully, they also take a long time to lose. For example, taking a month off from rigorous workouts creates a much steeper decline for an athlete than it does for a singer taking a month off of singing. That's great news for those seasons of life that require you to step away from your craft for a couple weeks to a month. In those time periods when you can't practice as intensely as you'd like, you'll likely maintain much of your previous technique without the fear of losing everything.

**To sing like never before**, don't become a slacker. But, do cut yourself some slack. This means knowing when to say: "Don't wake me! I'm practicing my singing!"

  **Prioritize sleep to assist in restoring your vocal health and expediting your vocal progress.**  **If you have many strenuous rehearsals, use marking as a tool for voice conservation.**  **Take a singing sabbath each week to recover from intense practices or performances.**

## 78 Top Ten Resolutions for Healthy Speech pt 1
## DON'T DROP THE BALL

11:59PM. New Years Eve. Manhattan. Zippers zip up. Snow sprinkles down. Any moment now, thousands of revelers will shout from "10" to "1." As they scream these ten digits with all the luster that their lungs can muster, let's hope they consider their vocal health.

Let's hope that their New Year's Resolutions are for Healthy Speech.

**HEALTHY SPEECH** means having a speaking voice that's sustainable not just for one evening, but for all 365 days of the year. Singers often make the mistake of training their singing voices year-round, while neglecting their speaking voices on a daily basis. Nevertheless, the speaking voice can become as healthy, reliable, and efficient as the singing voice. You can count on it!

### TEN! BREATHING

Breathing for healthy speech differs quite a bit from singing. In singing, multiple vocal registers and notes are often sustained for long durations. In speech, chest voice is most common, and spoken phrases are generally quite short in duration. Thus, speech requires a more audacious exhale in comparison to the more controlled breath support that singing requires. Your speech can be improved quickly and easily just by taking time to consciously prepare sufficient inhalations and begin your sentences with energetic exhalations.

### NINE! CONSONANTS

Singing always involves vocal fold vibrations. While speech mostly does too, did you ever consider that words can actually still be understood without the vocal folds phonating? For example, a series of crisp consonants can cause listeners to understand sentences without the vocal folds making a sound. In singing, the vowel's the thing. In speech, consonants are king! If consonants can help you to communicate ideas (with or without your vocal folds), then it's easy to see why better diction leads to healthy speech.

### EIGHT! CONFIDENCE

Sometimes speech problems are more mental than physical. The speaking voice can be compromised when a speaker perceives that something is wrong with them. This might manifest as a weak, hesitant, or restricted voice. Confidence transforms this issue when we discover that there's value not only in what we have to say, but also in who we are. Every person has a God-given voice, plus an opportunity to use their voice in valuable ways. Embracing this truth can help us transcend debilitating mental barriers.

**To sing like never before**, we don't have to wait until the next ball drops. Any day of the year can be the day that we make resolutions for improving our speaking habits. Let's not go another year dropping the ball on healthy speech!

---

 **SLNB QUICK TIPS**

**1** Improve your speaking voice by using committed and energetic exhalations.

**2** Speak with crisp consonants to improve the presence, clarity, and health of your voice.

**3** Remember that you are valuable and embrace the fact that your voice expresses this value.

As the moment approaches, some lovebirds just can't keep their eyes on the ball. Instead, they are homing in on that long-awaited New Year's kiss.

Unfortunately, it's never going to happen unless they learn to SPEAK UP!

### SEVEN! ALIGNMENT
Alignment problems and physical tension interfere with optimal breathing and the larynx's function. Perhaps the phone is constantly craning our necks. Maybe our jaws jut forward from hours at a computer screen. Or, what about the wear and tear of standing on our feet all day? Combating these issues might involve daily stretching, workouts, yoga, or Alexander technique. Regardless, we must find solutions for everyday tasks that jeopardize our alignment in order to improve healthy speech.

### SIX! IDENTITY
Vocalists usually attach their identity to a particular set of vocal characteristics. Whether or not these characteristics are produced healthfully, it's their voice nonetheless. One common example is someone with a naturally higher voice taxing their lower register because they think it sounds more mature. Of course, it's very important that we are comfortable with our vocal identity. However, it's even more important that we have healthy speech. Thankfully, after some training, vocalists are often pleased to discover that sounds that initially seemed to not be "them" later become their new identity. As you work on your voice, stay open to sounds that don't initially seem to be "you."

### FIVE! RESONANCE
The better the resonance, the healthier the speaking voice. Still, we often resist exploring our full capabilities because new resonances often seem unnatural. For example, lowering the larynx loosens the vocal folds and increases resonance space. However, we may initially perceive this as unusually dark and deep. Similarly, twang assists with projecting through spaces and crowds. However, we may perceive this as offensively bright and unpleasant. Experimenting with new resonances may seem unnatural to you at first, but it is essential for achieving healthy speech.

### FOUR! USAGE
Some professional athletes might train up to 3-5 hours in one day. But, what if this same athlete also walked for five more hours that same day? They would risk exhaustion or injury. In the same way, it's not always conscious vocal usage like practicing, rehearsing, or performing that leads to vocal problems. It's more often the unconscious vocal usage. How is your voice used at work? What about socially? Are there certain environments that compromise your vocal health? Healthy speech requires that we identify and correct our areas of imbalance or overuse.

**To sing like never before**, quit the cooing and start the wooing! If you've got love worth shouting from the rooftops, there are only three more seconds to SPEAK UP!

 Try disciplines like stretching, workouts, yoga, and Alexander technique to optimize alignment.

 Explore resonances that don't seem like "you." This helps maximize your voice's capabilities.

 Make a list of where you spend the most vocal energy. Do you need to make any adjustments?

# 80 Top Ten Resolutions for Healthy Speech pt 3 | Auld Things are Passed Away

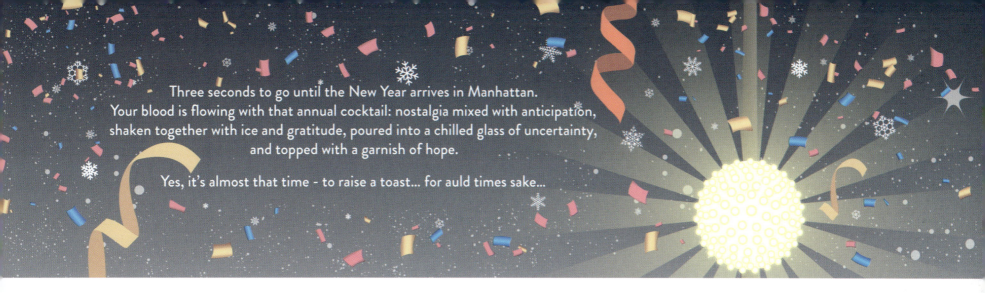

Three seconds to go until the New Year arrives in Manhattan. Your blood is flowing with that annual cocktail: nostalgia mixed with anticipation, shaken together with ice and gratitude, poured into a chilled glass of uncertainty, and topped with a garnish of hope.

Yes, it's almost that time - to raise a toast... for auld times sake...

### THREE! LOUD ENVIRONMENTS

Even with the best vocal technique, the voice is most susceptible to injury when it's asked to project in loud environments. One example is having to talk over the blaring music and raucous crowds of bars, clubs, and nightlife. Another might be a dance or fitness instructor competing with booming speakers. Still others include teachers speaking over unruly students or coaches yelling from the sidelines. Speaking in loud environments should be minimized whenever possible. However, when it cannot be avoided, monitoring your vocal technique and managing your fatigue levels becomes critical for healthy speech.

### TWO! VOCAL FRY

Vocal fry is the new black! That is, it's commonly considered culturally cool to speak with vocal fry. Yet, it can put your most healthy speech in the red. Vocal fry, by its nature, discourages airflow while also encouraging small amounts of compression. The result is speaking with very little assistance from the breath. While there's nothing inherently wrong with using vocal fry, overusing it can impede your most optimal speaking voice. So, don't fear the vocal fry, but don't overdo it just because it's cool!

### ONE! VARIETY

Many speaking voices can become quite monotone. They gravitate toward one pitch or a very small range of pitches. Unfortunately, using a limited speaking range is the equivalent of singing one musical pitch over and over again all day long. Any vocal task performed repeatedly and exclusively without variety and balance risks vocal fatigue. That's why healthy speech relies on vocal variety more than any other skill. Variety includes elements like pitch range, volume, vocal registers, compression, rhythm, inflection, and diction. In short, the more interesting your speaking voice is, the more likely it is to be healthy speech.

## HAPPY NEW VOICE!!!

**To sing like never before**, should auld acquaintance be forgot? Yes, they should! Especially if we've been acquainted with auld speaking habits that no longer serve our best vocal health. It's time to start fresh! So, make your resolutions, pucker up, and raise a glass! Your healthiest vocal years have just begun...

  Remain especially aware of your technique when having to speak in loud environments.  It isn't unhealthy to use vocal fry, but don't let it become your everyday speaking voice.  Use plenty of variety in your speaking voice to ensure both its longevity and interest.

# CHAPTER 9
*VOCAL PERFORMANCE & ACTING*

## 81 All Singers Are Actors

### SINGING'S PRAYER PARTNER

## LOOKING FOR ANSWERED PRAYERS? THEN SING!

As the famous saying goes: *"Singing is praying twice."*
What does this mean? It means that when we sing, there is soulfulness and life not only in our musicality, but also in the expression of our words. In effect, singing DOUBLES our artistic potential. That's why it's tragic when singers only pray "half a prayer." Didn't anyone ever tell them that

**ALL SINGERS ARE ACTORS?**

**ALL SINGERS ARE ACTORS** means that there is no singer who is JUST a singer. Sometimes singers make the mistake of focusing so hard on their vocal technique and musicality that they neglect the acting components of their craft. They may possess absolutely stunning instruments in terms of vocal technique—including an expansive range, powerful tone, impressive finesse, dexterous agility, and many other coveted abilities. Yet, while their skills are at elite levels—something is missing.

Conversely, there are singers who may have rather lackluster voices from a technical standpoint, yet they still manage to enthrall their listeners. In fact, some of these singers are among the most famous and beloved in all the world. How can such a phenomenon be explained?

It all comes down to the fact that there is a certain soulfulness, authenticity, and charisma that some singers possess. Although their technique might occasionally be flawed, it's always apparent that these artists know exactly what they are singing about. They've become masters of conveying spirit, emotion, and truth as they tell a story through song.

Unfortunately, too many singers resist embracing their acting capabilities by mistakenly believing that acting is only for Broadway and theatre singers. However, remember that acting for singing doesn't mean having to suddenly become showy or theatrical. *Acting for singing* means truthfully inhabiting, communicating, and expressing the meaning and emotion of a song's lyrics—in any musical style.

Ultimately, we should strive for both skills to complement one another. That is, our vocal technique should always enhance our acting abilities and vice versa. Whenever the beauty of any singing voice is met with an honest delivery of song lyrics, it's not just praying twice—it's an exponentially spiritual experience.

**To sing like never before**, we need to act like never before. Why hit notes when you can strike hearts? Why make music when you can make magic? Why sing from your lips when you can speak from your soul? These are all questions to pray about...

 If you call yourself a singer, then it's time to also start calling yourself a singing actor.

 To win your audience, think more about your soulful expression than your vocal technique.

 In all songs, strive to truthfully communicate the meaning, emotion, and story of the lyrics.

## 82 Identifying the Scene Partner — "You Talkin' to ME?"

**IDENTIFYING THE SCENE PARTNER** means deciding who you are talking to in a song. This concept seems rudimentary. Yet, singers who master it often appear to possess an uncanny ability to connect to their audiences: "It was like they were singing just to ME!"

Unfortunately, identifying the scene partner is commonly overlooked in the artistic process. The resulting error is evident in singers who generically sing to themselves. Or, those who sing to the crowd. Or, those who don't sing to anybody at all, but just simply sing.

Thankfully, identifying the scene partner is as simple as choosing a dear friend, a mortal enemy, a faithful lover, a cowardly cheat, a close family member, a mysterious stranger, a furry pet, the courageous part of yourself, or the insecure part of yourself. The person or part of yourself that you choose can be real or imaginary. However, the challenge comes in making sure your decision involves thought, creativity, and, most importantly—specificity.

The more specific you are about your scene partner, the more personal your performance will be. Your decision will drastically alter a song's meaning and delivery. Thus, it's vital that the scene partner you've chosen is someone who can best help you to make a meaningful connection to the lyrics.

Once you've made your choice, practice delivering your song lyrics as if they were being sung to your scene partner. When performance day arrives, don't just sing to yourself or to the audience. Instead, place your scene partner somewhere in the crowd's vicinity. Just as you used your imagination to create your scene partner, your audience will likewise begin to use their imaginations. They will instinctively see themselves as witnesses to the scene you've created. They will enjoy getting to experience the intimate conversation and genuine interaction you've established with your scene partner.

**To sing like never before**, you must sing to *someone* like never before! Everyone talks to themselves when nobody is watching. But, performers talk to themselves when *everyone* is watching. In either case, ask yourself an important question: "You talkin' to ME?!"

 With every song you sing, identify the scene partner by asking, "Who am I talking to?"

 Be specific with your choice. The more specific you are, the more personal your song will be.

 Place your scene partner in the audience's vicinity to help create a more intimate connection.

83 Playing the Action

| When the camera starts rolling, the Director is the only person who never forgets their lines. | The Director doesn't say  | The Director says  | That's because Directors know that good acting doesn't come from forcing flighty feelings. |  |

**PLAYING THE ACTION** means focusing performances on executing specific actions instead of feeling generic emotions. Actions can also be called "objectives" or "motivations." Playing the action is perhaps the most important principle in all of acting. In fact, that's why it's called "acting!"

Unfortunately, many performers end up playing the emotion instead of playing the action. This usually stems from the desire to give emotionally-driven performances. Yet, this well-intentioned desire is actually a trap. Performances focused on displaying emotions usually come across as emoting instead of as sincere acting. This often leaves audiences with the impression that the performance was forced, not believable, or even cheesy.

For this reason, it's essential to identify the primary action contained within a song's lyrics. Actions should be expressed as specific verbs. For instance, a love song may have the action "to woo" a lover. A grandiose ballad may be " to inspire" a legion of downtrodden people. A lament song may be "to heal" from a painful event.

To illustrate, let's look at the classic song "Over the Rainbow." It's typically very tempting to sing this timeless tune with a sort of hackneyed heartache or wishy-washy wistfulness—getting caught up in the cloying clichés of lemon drops and lullabies. But, upon thorough investigation of the lyrics…

**"If happy, little bluebirds fly above the rainbow—why then, oh why can't I?"**

… we quickly discover that the song is actually about overcoming disbelief and doubt. Perhaps we can imagine that our scene partner is someone who denies the existence of the beautiful land beyond the rainbow. Our action could be "to overcome" their disbelief or even "to convince" them that it's real.

Instantaneously, the performance is no longer generic. Instead, it becomes drama—with desires, consequences, and purpose. The emotions still remain palpable within the singing, music, and lyrics. Yet, there is no longer any need to play the emotions. They present themselves organically as byproducts of the action instead.

**To sing like never before**, our performances must not be a hopeless jumble of feelings. Instead, we must find truth and sincerity by playing the action. So, don't search for emotions somewhere in the clouds. Let actions keep your performances grounded!

 |  Instead of seeking the emotion of the song, seek the song's action, purpose, or objective. |  Express your actions as verbs. For example, "to persuade," "to seduce," or "to inspire." |  Focus on playing the action, and your emotions will become organic and unforced.

**PLAYING THE OPPOSITE** means to intentionally work against audience expectations. By playing into expectations, performers forfeit the element of surprise. By playing the opposite, performers gain a tremendous advantage in terms of capturing attention.

For example, comedic scenes may tempt actors to perform in funny or hammy ways. The sound of chirping crickets is usually the result. On the other hand, if comedic scenes are played in serious or deadpan ways, then the audience becomes much more likely to laugh.

Similarly, heavy dramatic scenes may tempt actors to perform in sad or melancholic ways. If this is the case, then the audience is probably in for a very long evening of watching the actor emote. Yet, if the actor battles to regain hope through their sadness, then the audience may find themselves emotional instead.

Playing the opposite isn't about avoiding performing scenes in obvious ways. It's about actively seeking out opposite choices. Here's a little chart with some examples. In each scenario, we start with a character's action. Then, we look at the obvious way to play the action. Finally, we see the opposite way it might be played:

| ACTION | OBVIOUS | OPPOSITE |
|---|---|---|
| Villain seeks to harm | Evil and sinister | Giddy and enthusiastic |
| Lover expresses feelings | Happy and gushing | Awed and incredulous |
| Wife scolds husband | Yells and screams | Smiles and talks sweetly |
| Victim seeks healing | Cries and sobs | Fights for courage and strength |
| Hero promises victory | Loud and bombastic | Calm and convinced |

In each of these scenarios, the performer's allure increases tremendously. The villain appears psychotic and twisted. The lover seems charming and authentic. The wife comes across as comically condescending. The victim becomes sympathetic. The hero sounds sincere and humble. Playing the opposite makes performances of all kinds more compelling by adding depth and dimension to scenes and characters.

**To sing like never before**, don't just do what your audience expects. Do the opposite! After all, didn't this chapter's title make you read a little more closely? Ahem…

 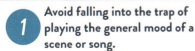 **1** Avoid falling into the trap of playing the general mood of a scene or song. 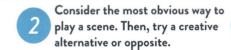 **2** Consider the most obvious way to play a scene. Then, try a creative alternative or opposite. 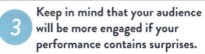 **3** Keep in mind that your audience will be more engaged if your performance contains surprises.

## 85 · Song Monologue Work

"...THAT IS THE QUESTION!"

"WHETHER 'TIS NOBLER IN THE MIND TO SUFFER THE SLINGS AND ARROWS OF OUTRAGEOUS ACTING CHOICES."

"OR, TO TAKE ARMS AGAINST A SEA OF VOCAL HABITS AND, BY OPPOSING - END THEM!"

Often we're so concerned about notes, rhythms, style, and technique that we forget completely about the meaning of our lyrics. Thankfully, we can borrow from the Bard by turning our songs into Monologues!

**SONG MONOLOGUE WORK** is a discipline in which song lyrics are taken out of their musical context entirely and treated purely as text. Although the concept is very simple, most singers find song monologue work to be quite challenging.

Absent of the beauty and emotion of their melodic and rhythmic context, song lyrics almost always sound naked at first. Yet, "there's the rub!" Song monologue work forces us to make artistic choices based on our words instead of the music.

### "Though this be madness, yet there is method in it!"

The method is as easy as these five acts:

**I—WRITE THE LYRICS**. Make sure that the lyrics are written in a completely isolated format so that you're not influenced by the music in any way.

**II—SPEAK THE LYRICS**. Do this as flatly and plainly as possible. Try to totally eliminate the melody and rhythms from your delivery as if the text were words and not song lyrics.

**III—ACT THE LYRICS**. Being careful to not revert back to the song's melody and rhythms, speak the words with the feeling and interpretation of an acting monologue. This should sound like a very sincere delivery of text.

**IV—ACT THE MELODY**. Keep the emotion, timing, and pace of the monologue that you've created, but with the melody added back. Don't worry about rhythms at this point. Just add the pitches. This should sound like an expressive conversation that just happens to be on pitch.

**V—ACT THE SONG**. Add back the tempo or the accompaniment. The song should sound normal once again. However, a new arsenal of acting choices, phrasing ideas, word emphases, rhythmic variety, style, and character are now available to you.

Once you've completed these five acts, nobody can accuse you of being "just a singer" ever again. Instead, you have become an interpreter of song!

**To sing like never before**, song monologue work's the thing! Our lyrics should never be an "undiscovered country." If they are, then we must "shuffle off this melodic coil." To speak. To sing. Perchance to dream...

 Try speaking the words of any song as though they are the text of a monologue.

 Be sure to not revert to the rhythms or melody of the song, but instead use plain speech.

 Allow song monologue work to influence how you act, phrase, and feel your song.

Did you know that the word for **BREATH** and the word for **SPIRIT** are the SAME?

In Latin, the word **"SPIRITUS"** simultaneously means **"BREATH"** and **"SPIRIT"**.

To "inspire" **"INSPIRARE"** means to **"BREATHE IN"** but also to **"FILL WITH CREATIVE SPIRIT"**.

To "expire" **"EXPIRARE"** means to **"BREATHE OUT"** but also to **"BRING TO AN END"**.

This comes as no surprise to singers. Singers understand that their voices are connected to a very deep and perhaps even spiritual part of themselves.

Thus, whenever Breath and Spirit become one, singers breathe LIFE into their performances!

---

**BREATHING THE PERFORMANCE** means merging the breath with the soulful aspects of a song. It's easy to emphasize breathing during technique practice, only to neglect it when it comes to performance. Thankfully, we can learn to breathe the performance by understanding how our breath can connect with our mind, body, soul, and spirit.

## MIND
Breathing the performance begins with the practical step of deciding where to *breathe* in every song. It's wise to consider and plan your breaths in advance. Whenever possible, breaths should come after periods, commas, or ends of ideas. This helps to best communicate the meaning of the lyrics to the audience.

## BODY
Physical tension is common during performances due to nerves, pressure, or anxiety. This tension can be greatly alleviated simply by completing every expiration (thereby releasing the diaphragm). Make sure each breath, thought, and phrase is brought to an end without rushing to the next inhalation. Completing your exhalations offers your body constant opportunities for relaxation. You can even try a nice complete exhalation right now! See how calming that feels?

## SOUL
To connect to a song's inner life, imagine that you breathe in the next lyric as you inhale. Similarly, imagine that you breathe out that same lyric as you sing. Each inspiration inspires the thought, while each expiration completes the thought. This practice ensures that every phrase you sing is grounded with intention, purpose, and meaningful expression.

## SPIRIT
Your audience desires to be moved and inspired by your performance. Yet, you don't have to manufacture a spiritual experience for them. You just have to remember that breath from your lips creates sound waves that travel to your audience. Thus, your audience inspires the breath and spirit that you've expired. In that sense, there's nothing we can do to stop singing from being a spiritual experience on some level. It's just a matter of learning to trust and embrace this as artists. Singing is the art of giving spirit to others.

**To sing like never before**, breath and spirit must become one and the same. If you learn to breathe the performance, you will take your audience's breath away. More importantly, they will take away yours.

---

**SLNB QUICK TIPS**

1. Plan your breaths in a song to ensure that you make sense of the lyric and have enough air.
2. To reduce tension, complete each phrase's exhalation without rushing to the next inhalation.
3. Allow each inhalation to inspire your thought, and each exhalation to complete your thought.

## 87 TRYING TO MAKE A GOOD IMPRESSION

*that still, small voice*

You enjoy a blockbuster action film every once in awhile. Yet, you'll always go back to that home movie of mom unwrapping your surprise gift.

You sometimes vacation to the world's most exotic destinations. Yet, the old oak that grew up with you still sways in your memories.

You notice the heartthrob on the magazine rack. Yet, you'll forever sigh for that girl next door with the sideways grin, or your kindhearted prince with the dimpled chin.

It's true… the cannonball makes the biggest splash. Yet, your feet splashing in the sunset's sand somehow make the deeper impression.

**TRYING TO MAKE A GOOD IMPRESSION** occurs when performers try too hard to please their audience. It's instinctive for all people to want others to like us—whether it's on a first date, a job interview, or talking to strangers. Our initial thought is usually: "How can I make a good impression?"

Unfortunately, the good impression that we try to make is rarely our true self. Instead, it's a role that we're temporarily playing. It's an illusion that we want others to see, instead of who we truly are. While this instinct is natural, almost nothing could be more stifling to an artist!

Art imitates life. Thus, to truly live as an artist is to reveal our humanity. Errors, flaws, and idiosyncrasies are all facets of our humanness. It's quite liberating to embrace the fact that these imperfections make our performances better, not worse.

Industry professionals often pride themselves on being unimpressed. Casting directors, agents, managers, and music executives have viewed thousands of auditions and performances and have already seen it all. Generally, they're not interested in people showing off or trying to prove themselves. They're looking instead for performers whose artistry is truthful, original, and authentic. Interestingly, though, this is also true for audiences who may know almost nothing about music. Even laypeople know instinctively when performers are "real" and when they're "faking it."

**To sing like never before**, consider this: Which voice has made the greatest impression on your life? Was it the showboaty shout of some starlet? Or, was it the soulful susurrations of someone who sincerely supports your journey? Similarly, in singing, it's not always impressiveness that impresses. Instead, it's the courage to give yourself. It's the daring to be different. It's the bravery to allow your best sounds to always remain a still, small voice.

**SLNB QUICK TIPS**

1. Think of people or situations in your life and your art that are asking for more of the "real you."
2. Remember that flaws and idiosyncrasies can very often make you more interesting and likable.
3. Your ability to impress will never be as impressive as your ability to be yourself.

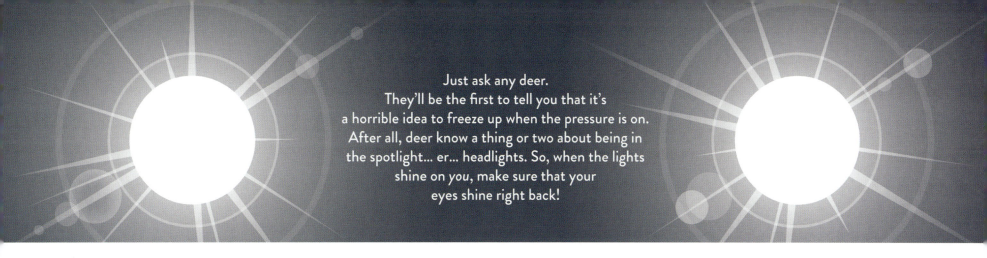

Just ask any deer.
They'll be the first to tell you that it's
a horrible idea to freeze up when the pressure is on.
After all, deer know a thing or two about being in
the spotlight... er... headlights. So, when the lights
shine on you, make sure that your
eyes shine right back!

**SINGING FROM THE EYES** is the sensation that the voice is being produced from the eyes themselves. Obviously nobody can actually sing from their eyes. However, the imagery and visualization of this is often highly effective for performers, both artistically and technically.

Artistically, skilled performers recognize that they can convey far more with their eyes than with the rest of their face. Although the face is bigger in size, even subtle movements of the eyes can convey powerful emotion and truth like no other part of the body.

Technically, the eyes can play a role in assisting with resonance. The eyes are located above the cheekbones and on both sides of the nose. When emphasizing head resonance and nasal resonance, it's very common for singers to experience physical sensations in the cheekbones, nose, and forehead. Thus, imagining the voice emanating from the eyes is a practical strategy for integrating resonance and technical sensations into an expressive performance.

Anytime a performer is disconnected from the intention, meaning, and emotion of their performance, their eyes are literally a dead giveaway. The extreme of this is the proverbial deer in the headlights expression. More commonly, though, eyes appear lifeless, locked, or vacant. This happens whenever a performer is thinking too hard about what they sound like, look like, or what their audience is thinking about them.

An amazingly simple, yet transformative performance trick is to *allow the eyes to actually see*. When rehearsing, auditioning, or performing, try calmly observing objects in the room or on the stage. Allow the eyes to simply take in the space—to truly see. Almost as if by magic, this discipline will cause you to instantly look and feel at home—even in your most high-pressure performance environment. A present and settled countenance in the eyes is often the final barrier standing between a performer and their greatest performance.

**To sing like never before**, we must be willing to roll down the windows to our souls and allow our eyes to sing the truth. Will you be a performer perpetually frozen in the headlights? Nay! Not when you realize... the EYES have it!

**1** Before singing a song, take a moment to allow your eyes to truly see your environment.

**2** Practice seeing your environment as a means of helping you to feel at home as you perform.

**3** Anytime you feel nervous or lose your focus, bring yourself back to singing from the eyes.

## 89 NERVES & PERFORMANCE ANXIETY

STRESS & SKIVVIES

## NERVES AND PERFORMANCE ANXIETY

**NERVES AND PERFORMANCE ANXIETY** occur when a performer experiences stress or nervousness either before or during a performance. If that's you, you're not alone. Virtually every performer suffers from nerves and performance anxiety at some point on their vocal journey. In fact, some of the world's most renowned singers still get nervous before performances.

Thankfully, there are many effective strategies for reducing nerves. Some of them include breathing exercises, meditation, yoga, stretching, pre-performance rituals, and affirmations. However, while all of these strategies can certainly help, the real question is: Do we actually want to rid ourselves of nerves in the first place?

Let's think about what nerves actually are. *Nerves* refer to the nervous system or the brain. Nerves are fibers that send messages from the brain to various muscles about what the body should do. Experiencing nervousness isn't necessarily a bad thing. It's actually a form of excitement. It demonstrates that we care deeply about our performance and that we're thinking about it—a lot!

Consider the concept of potential energy vs. kinetic energy in physics. *Potential energy* is stored up energy. *Kinetic energy* is energy in motion.

Nerves are comparable to potential energy. Having more stored-up energy is actually advantageous. It just means we have more energy! However, if this potential energy isn't converted into kinetic energy, then we feel as tightly-wound as a coil spring.

Nerves are often sparked by thoughts like: "Will I sound good enough?", "Will the audience like me?" or "Will I be successful?" But questions like these are out of our control and are impossible to answer. So, they keep thoughts trapped as nervous potential energy.

Instead, focus your nervous energy toward thoughts like: "What story do I want to tell?" "What are my acting intentions?" or "What meaning am I giving to the lyrics?" Questions like these convert nervous energy into action. Ultimately, changing your focus in this way causes performances to turn out better than they would have without any nerves.

**To sing like never before**, it's wise to avoid visualizing your audience nearing a strip poker defeat. Why waste all your energy on stress and skivvies? Especially when being nervous can be of such great service!

  Keep in mind that your nerves can actually be more of a blessing than a curse.  Avoid focusing on unanswerable questions and things that are out of your control.  Channel your nerves into performance energy, storytelling, honest lyrics, and acting choices.

## 90 LIVING IN THE MOMENT — I'M NOT KINDLING!

If you're trying to build a fire, then you'll need kindling. What is kindling? Nothing more than a bunch of dead wood, really. Yet, if you want a breathtaking blaze, then you're going to need lots of it. The more kindling you accumulate, the more your fire will incinerate.

Still, without a SPARK - all you've got is dead wood...

**LIVING IN THE MOMENT** means minimizing technical concentration in order to maximize true artistry. This doesn't mean you should sacrifice good vocal technique. In fact, the greater your technique, the greater your artistic potential. However, technique by itself is merely dead wood without the fiery life that can only be stoked in the moment...

## LIVE PREPAREDLY

With the exception of improvisational singing, songs should be rehearsed until their requirements can be performed on autopilot. This includes melodies, rhythms, lyrics, breathing decisions, acting choices, stylistic nuances, and technical details. Preparation is a prerequisite to living in the moment.

## LIVE SPONTANEOUSLY

Each day, we are different people, artists, and singers. So, each performance that we give will be different too. It's tempting to try to duplicate past performances that were successful. It's also tempting to plan how we think upcoming performances should go. Unfortunately, it's impossible to recreate the past or have the future go exactly as we imagine. Instead of planning, allow each performance to be its own little surprise.

## LIVE TRUSTINGLY

While it takes a measure of faith, every singer must eventually learn to let go and trust their technique. This can be a challenge for those who enjoy controlling, analyzing, and refining their craft. Ultimately, though, too much critical thinking is like throwing a bucket of water on your fire. You can't judge yourself and live in the moment at the same time.

## LIVE WISELY

All fires can rage out of control at times. So, it's not a crime to think about technique occasionally during performance. If a difficult note or phrase is feeling troublesome, then it's wise to temporarily shift to a technical focus. Once you're certain that the blaze has been contained, then go right back to basking in the glow!

**To sing like never before**, our performances shouldn't be stiff as a log. They should be constantly consuming conflagrations. Prepare well. Be open to surprises. Trust your technique. Attend to unexpected wildfires. If you do, then your audience will cozy up to you—alive in that precious fleeting moment—with spirits kindled by the flame that forever flickers in your soul.

**1** Ask yourself if your performing has become too technical and lacks a certain spark.

**2** Transition from technical concentration to true artistry by learning to live in the moment.

**3** To live in the moment, make sure to prepare well, be spontaneous, and trust your technique.

# CHAPTER 10
*SINGING FROM THE SOUL*

## 91 Taking the First Step

**FORGET THE DIFFERENCE**

An ancient Proverb by Lao Tzu tells us:

## The journey of 1,000 Miles begins with a single step.

A new Vocal Proverb tells us:

## The vocal journey is difficult to begin, but impossible to end.

With a single step or a single note, something special starts anytime we dare to Take The First Step...

**TAKING THE FIRST STEP** is among the most daunting challenges, both in singing and in life. We are often so imprisoned by procrastination, fear, doubt, and perfectionism that we avoid pursuing our deepest desires and purest passions.

However, there is one thing that almost all people have in common—the need to sing. This need must triumph over our fears. So, whether you're an advanced singer, a complete beginner, or a shower singer, take these first steps to begin your journey of 1,000 high notes...

## STUDY

Find a voice teacher that you trust. Not every teacher is right for every singer. However, if you find one who understands your goals and can help you achieve them, then there are few things as gratifying as becoming a lifelong student of singing. Many of the greatest singers and voice teachers still study voice on a regular basis with their trusted teacher or coach.

## LISTEN

Create a listening regimen. Listen to artists that you love while also stretching yourself to other genres, time periods, and possibilities. Don't just listen passively like a fan, but listen actively like an artist. See if you can mimic some of the stylistic gestures that you hear. Listening intelligently and intentionally can transform your technique, style, and artistry.

## PRACTICE

Practice is a discipline, but it doesn't have to feel like one. Whether short or long, relaxed or intense, formal or informal, practice should never be a chore. Instead, it should be satisfying, sustainable, and something you look forward to each day. On days that you don't feel like doing a long practice session, try to do just a little bit anyway. You'll leave feeling better than you did before and thankful that you at least checked in with your voice.

## SHARE

Your voice is a gift that's meant to be shared. If you're a shy singer, then try dedicating some of your private singing to somebody you care about or to somebody who has passed on. If you're a more confident singer, then start finding your audience, large or small. Either way, it's critical that your voice does not remain bottled up inside you. There will always be *someone* who needs to hear you sing.

**To live like never before**, we must audaciously take the first step...

An ancient proverb by Martin Luther tells us:

### "As long as we live, there is never enough singing."

A new vocal proverb tells us:

### "As long as we sing, there is always enough life."

Start singing... Start living... Start forgetting the difference.

---

**SLNB QUICK TIPS**

1. Take the first step by trying a lesson with a trusted Voice Teacher.
2. Take the first step by creating a listening regimen or a daily practice routine.
3. Take the first step by sharing your singing with someone you love (even if it's not perfect).

## 92 — Am I Too Old to Sing?

The Old Man & the Glee

**"AM I TOO OLD TO SING?"** is a question asked by singers of all ages. Yet, questioning the right age to sing is like questioning the right age to be happy. If we're not careful, an entire lifetime of questions can keep us from singing.

### AGE 4-11
*"Is singing something that a child can actually do seriously?"* It's easy to dismiss a young person's interest in singing. Many children sing naturally, freely, and with no inhibitions. So, singing is often thought to be a mere inevitability of childhood, as opposed to a legitimate craft or talent.

### AGE 12-16
*"Isn't it best to wait until his voice is fully mature?"* The voice changes quite a bit during puberty. As a result, teenagers are frequently doubted when their developing voices are in flux. However, the teen years are actually a very fruitful time to train the voice. It's also a time where young people have an opportunity to build confidence, identity, and positive self-expression through their singing.

### AGE 17-22
*"I missed my chance to be a superstar, so what's the point of trying?"* By the late teen years, young adults frequently compare themselves to stars who've already achieved big success by their age. While it may sound comical, it's actually quite common for young people in this age group to believe that they are too old to sing.

### AGE 20-39
*"How can I even think of my singing dreams with everything so busy at work?"* For people in their twenties and thirties, singing often seems like an impractical hobby that's too far removed from career life. They frequently find themselves too busy with other priorities to spend time on their artistic side.

### AGE 40-59
*"Shouldn't I put my family's interests ahead of my own?"* Folks in their forties and fifties frequently find themselves too focused on family life to entertain their desire to sing. The opportunity to sing seems like a missed chance that ought to be given to the younger generation.

### AGE 60-100+
Fortunately, in their later years, many people pursue their deepest passions after reflecting on what matters most. They realize that it is never too late to sing. They take up singing lessons, join choral groups, and discover their voices in ways that they never thought possible: *"I feel younger than ever. How can I keep from singing?"*

There will always be countless questions that we can ask ourselves. But, as you can see, most of these questions only cause us to put our passions on hold for another day. Or another year. Or another decade. So, if you find yourself asking "Am I too old to sing?" maybe try replacing it with a different question: "What am I waiting for?"

**To sing like never before**, singing should be the one gift that we never quite grow into and we never outgrow. If age is "just a number," then singing is the best way to lose count.

**1** Speak your age to yourself out loud right now. You've just told yourself the perfect age to sing.

**2** Strive to filter out the negative comments of doubters and naysayers. Your voice is your own.

**3** Isn't it better to go after what you are passionate about now than to have regrets later?

 93 Singing Is a Sport

**"SINGING IS A SPORT"** is a popular adage which suggests that vocal training is similar to athletic training. Maybe the most debilitating lie singers are told is this: "You have to be born with it." This lie has robbed untold vocalists of the confidence and courage to develop their voices. Thankfully, one of the best remedies is to remember that singing is a sport.

In truth, singing requires as much muscular training as any sport. We've explored numerous examples of how vocal technique involves respiratory, laryngeal, glottal, facial, and postural muscles. From beginner to elite professional, all singers must train like athletes for their vocal muscles to become coordinated, efficient, and reliable.

Nevertheless, it's common for aspiring singers to hear reactions like:

*"You're training your voice? Can you even do that?"*
*"You either have talent, or you don't."*
*"Some people are just tone deaf."*
*"So what do you plan to DO with your singing?"*
*"Well, just don't quit your day job!"*

Only a small percentage of athletes ever achieve a professional sporting career. Yet, the health benefits of physical activity are universally recognized. It's common knowledge that athletics improve energy, mental clarity, and emotional well-being. Our bodies were made to be active and strong.

Likewise, only a small percentage of singers ever achieve a professional singing career. Sadly though, many non-professional singers miss out on the gift of singing because they become deceived and discouraged by negative words. In response to this, the idea that singing is a sport offers a simple, yet powerful truth: *The voice can and must be trained.* This truth trumps the all too common misunderstanding that singing is something that you need to be born with. It also empowers singers to receive the extraordinary physical, emotional, mental, and spiritual benefits that only the sport of singing can offer.

**To sing like never before,** you don't have to be born with anything except an unyielding passion to sing. Your body is a temple. Sports may keep its walls strong—but only singing can fill its halls with your soul's sweetest song. Play on.

 Reject the lie that singing is something that you must be born with.

 Think of training your voice just like training your body. In reality, there are very few differences.

 Enjoy the countless benefits of singing, even if you don't intend to pursue it professionally.

## 94 Vocal Friendship

Can you solve this riddle?

I've been with you since before you can remember. I've been a comfort in your cruelest heartbreaks and an ally to your gladdest victories. I've never asked anything of you, even though you've sometimes asked much of me. Every time you express the deepest parts of yourself, I am there with you. I will never leave you as long as you can utter one word.

**VOCAL FRIENDSHIP** means that singing is more than a mere set of skills and abilities. Instead, singing is a constant and faithful companion throughout your life's journey. What a tragedy to mistake your best friend for yet another business partner.

Still, many hopeful singers find themselves asking: "How long will singing take? How many months or years will I need? Will I have to spend resources, time, or effort on training? What if I pursue singing and never get what I want out of it?"

While these are all valid questions, they are ultimately the *wrong* questions. Asking questions like these is like asking a friend to sign a terms and conditions contract before you spend time together. *Ask not what singing can do for you—ask what friendship can do for your singing.*

Friendships aren't transactional. Friendships are transformative. Friendships driven by obligations, burdens, and expectations can never become quality friendships. Likewise, singing isn't transactional. Singing is transcendent. That's why it is self-defeating to impose rigid deadlines, demands, and pressure onto our singing. Of course, it is very positive to set goals. However, singing should ideally transcend our biggest goals and ambitions.

Singing might make you a success. It might become your career. It might even turn you into a global sensation. But, regardless of whether it does any of these things—singing can teach you how to love yourself. Perhaps that's why singing is a friend unlike any other. Your vocal friendship offers you a lifetime of opportunities to appreciate who you really are. *To love your voice is to love yourself.*

**To sing like never before**, we must persevere through times when life feels like a riddle. Those forlorn hours when it seems like every friend has abandoned us. Even on that coldest, bleakest, and most desolate night... SING. As your breath turns to fog against the bitter night air, suddenly you'll see the answer. Before your very eyes... you've got a friend who sticks closer than a brother.

  Ask yourself a serious question: "Do I have a good relationship with my own voice?"  Avoid placing so many demands on your vocal progress that you lose your love of singing.  Thank your voice for all the times that it has been there for you in meaningful ways.

## STICKS AND STONES MAY BREAK MY BONES...

If none of these exact words were ever said to you, then certainly you recall some other painful words that have affected your singing. Write them down in your book (go ahead - it's therapeutic!):

"_____"

If you had nothing to write, then you are a rare singer indeed. For virtually ALL singers are recovering from Vocal Scars.

**VOCAL SCARS** are psychological or emotional wounds resulting from destructive words in a singer's past. Sadly, criticism is handed out far more liberally than encouragement. As a consequence, many singers carry vocal scars left by family, teachers, friends, enemies, or even strangers.

The voice is inseparable from our identity and sense of self. Thus, criticizing the voice cuts deeper than an everyday insult. It undermines a person's expression of their individuality. Thankfully, there are several ways we can heal from vocal scars.

### FORGIVENESS
Forgiveness never means excusing another person's actions. Forgiveness means letting go of hurt done to us. Make certain that you've forgiven anyone who has negatively impacted your voice.

### SUPPORT
If possible, distance yourself from unsupportive environments. Find a core group of people that value your vocal journey. True love means cherishing someone's voice—even when (especially when) it's not perfect.

### RIGHTS
Your voice belongs to you and nobody else. You have a God-given right to sing. Don't forget that no person or unkind word can ever take that from you.

### PERSPECTIVE
As human beings, it's common for us to receive a thousand praises and still dwell on one negative remark. Remember to value and cherish the positive words that have been said about your voice.

### MOTIVATION
Ironically, singing can help us heal from pain about... singing! Don't let someone's negative words silence you. Use them as motivation to sing with more passion, fire, and devotion than ever!

**To sing like never before**, cross out what you wrote above and write the truth:

"_____"

If you need help, then try: **"I love my voice." "I love to sing." "My voice is one-of-a-kind." "Nobody will ever keep me from singing." "I can achieve my singing goals."**

Your vocal scars don't define you. Your soul defines you. So, will you allow negative words to ring in your ears? Or will the courageous sounds of your own precious singing drown them out?

### ...BUT MY VOICE WILL ALWAYS HEAL ME.

---

  Even if it's difficult, work on forgiving those who have hurt you on your vocal journey.  Try not to dwell on one negative comment when there are many positives about your voice.  Seek out a small and trustworthy network of people who support you and your singing.

# 96 PERFECTIONISM — BLESS THIS MESS

**PERFECTIONISM** is the psychological desire to avoid failure at all costs. While it's not unique to the arts, perfectionism is perhaps the biggest enemy of the true artist. The pursuit of excellence should not be confused with perfectionism. It occurs when unrealistic expectations are placed upon the pursuit of excellence. Ironically, there is one fundamental mistake that keeps all perfectionists from ever being perfect—forgetting how important our failures are.

## FAILURE IS LEARNING

Many valuable life lessons are impossible to learn without failure. If we quit when something becomes difficult, then we can never grow. Almost every human achievement—from science to technology to medicine to politics to music—has been won through a series of trials... and errors. Without failure, we can never realize our fullest potential. In a certain sense, the greater our failures, the greater our potential for success.

## FAILURE IS HUMAN

To err is human. There is not a single person who is without fault. In fact, the more closely we examine ourselves, the more faults we see. Perfectionists are often so fixated on their flaws that they become desperate to correct them or cover them up. But, again—to err is human!

Perfectionism robs us of our very humanity. It denies us our chance to discover how loved we are. Not *in spite of* our humanity, but *because* of it.

## FAILURE IS ART

Art is the creative expression of our humanity. So, it makes sense why art that is ostensibly imperfect is the art that humans often cherish most dearly. Conversely, perfect art is either boring or isn't considered art at all. Singing is the only art form where humans are the musical instrument. So, singing might just be the best way to finally embrace the beauty of failure.

**To sing like never before**, dare to be a mess. Perhaps the greatest tragedy of perfectionism is that many artists believe that their pursuit of perfection will make them successful—when it's actually the only thing standing in their way. Don't miss out on the growth, the humanity, the artistry, and the love that only a total failure can experience.

 **1** Consider your most recent failure. What lessons did you draw from this experience? **2** Think about your favorite singer. Are there any flaws that you adore in this person's artistry? **3** Let singing teach you not only that it's okay to fail, but that failure is among life's best gifts.

**SINGING IS A GIFT** means that our voices cannot be earned, cannot be held, and can only be given away. Yet, some singers develop the chronic and debilitating habit of deriding their own voices. This can happen to professional singers as easily as it can to beginners. Accolades, victories, and compliments are often no match for the intense self-loathing and discontent created by this condition. Constant negativity towards one's own voice eventually leads to confidence problems, decreased progress, and a loss of the fun of singing. Thankfully, much of this can be remedied by remembering that singing is a gift...

## TO YOU
When you receive a gift from someone, it would be unthinkably rude to scoff at it. Instead, you express gratitude for having received something that's meant just for you. Think about it—your voice is one of the greatest gifts you'll ever receive. While it may not be exactly as you'd wish, it's still a gift intended especially for you. Awe and gratitude triumph over negativity anytime we remember just how fortunate we are to sing in the first place.

## TO OTHERS
We don't give gifts to impress others. We give gifts to make others happy. Yet, we're often unwilling to share our singing until it's impressive enough. Singing to impress acutely amplifies nerves, pressure, and performance anxiety. Whenever performances are intended as displays of skillfulness, fear intensifies. Whenever performances are intended as gifts, fear diminishes.

## TO THE WORLD
No singing voice is an accident. Nevertheless, it's very easy to believe that our voices are unimportant and insignificant. Consider this though: if you use your voice positively for just *one* other person, then you'll have forever impacted the world. Never underestimate the goodness that can be done through your voice—even with its flaws!

**To sing like never before**, old precedents of negativity must be broken. Your voice is not an ugly duckling. Your voice is a gift. If you believe this, then self-hatred, fear, and doubt will roll off you like water off a duck's back!

  Because your voice is a gift to you, you can learn to cherish it more than you disparage it.  Because your voice is a gift to others, you can become fearless about sharing it.  Because your voice is a gift to the world, you can appreciate that it has great significance.

## 98 "Making It" as a Singer — If Joy Shines...

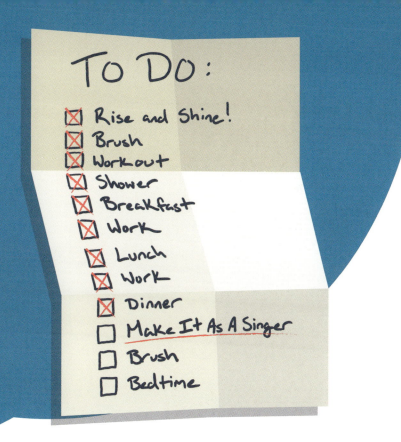

Sadly, the myth of making it gives artists the false impression that artistic satisfaction is something that can be completed. Almost as if it can be checked off of some ultimate to-do list. The truth is, accomplishments, jobs, finances, and awards aren't equipped to leave us feeling complete.

This misconception doesn't just plague big stars. Beginners, vocal students, parents, voice teachers, and budding professionals often make the same mistake. That is, to value making it over the craft of singing. To place achievement ahead of art. To cherish product over process. To make goals more important than joy.

Of course, goals are quite positive, generally speaking. Setting goals inspires hard work, determination, and focus. However, people begin to suffer when goals become idolized as ultimate things. This breeds disappointment, both during failure *and* during success. In failure, heartbreak is followed by feelings of: "I'm worthless." In success, fleeting triumph is followed by feelings of: "Now what?"

It's essential to understand that we can never "arrive." This shouldn't discourage us, but should instead cause us to perpetually thrive! If you succeed at a goal, don't let it be your last. If you fail at a goal, cheerfully move forward by setting a new one. Let your goals inspire your vocal journey and not overtake it. Making it is temporary. Making art is eternal.

**To sing like never before**, making it shouldn't make it onto your to-do list. Sometimes the flickering flashbulbs of stardom may pave your path down the red carpet. Other times, the lonely bulb of your studio apartment may be the sole spark still celebrating your sincerest sounds. If joy shines in both places, then you've truly… made it.

**"MAKING IT" AS A SINGER** is the elusive goal of attaining a permanent state of artistic accomplishment, satisfaction, or security. Unfortunately, "making it" is an illusion and isn't tangibly achievable. As a consequence, many artists suffer as they strive in vain towards the myth of making it.

It's all too common to learn of celebrity artists who reach the pinnacle of success only to be left with the crippling feeling of: "Is this it?" Drugs, depression, and legal problems often accompany this phenomenon. But why? Shouldn't someone who is winning awards, earning millions of fans, and receiving lavish attention be satisfied to have made it?

**1** If you fail at one of your goals, don't dwell on the failure. Move quickly to a new one!

**2** If you succeed at one of your goals, don't let it be a stopping point. Keep growing!

**3** To really make it as a singer, take joy in your singing regardless of your circumstances.

 99 The Vocal Journey

**THE VOCAL JOURNEY** is the pursuit of the inseparable bond that our inner lives share with our singing. You have may noticed a very interesting phenomenon. That is, when you take a leap forward in your vocal life, your inner life blossoms as well. Similarly, when you develop as a person, your singing seems to improve as if by magic. This is no coincidence!

Your vocal journey will reveal that you cannot separate your inner life from your singing, even if you try. As your life evolves, begin to witness how your victories and setbacks manifest themselves in your singing voice. As your singing evolves, begin to witness how your life is forever altered by the sounds you make. Chances are, you'll marvel at the effect your personal development has on your singing. High notes have fewer high stakes. Challenging repertoire is conquered with newfound confidence and composure. Even your tone itself evokes the emotion of every experience that you've enjoyed or endured.

Most importantly, though, your vocal journey will exhibit the endless ways that singing is transformative. Your comfort zone will be completely rezoned with courage. Passion will become the new medium to replace your tedium. You might even smile the kind of smile that your face has always hoped you'd smile.

Even in those times when singing is a struggle, your voice is still a profound truth teller. It illuminates pain, insecurity, and doubts that have hibernated in the caverns of your consciousness for years. Thankfully though, singing never unearths a wound without also being the catalyst for its healing. Singing is meant to repair, rejuvenate, and restore your most broken places. Your voice can literally heal you from within.

**To sing like never before**, practice makes perfect. But, don't just practice singing so that you can be a better singer. Practice singing so that you can truly live. After all, it's not the destination... it's the vocal journey.

**1** As you develop as a person, observe vocal growth happening in unexpected ways.

**2** As you develop as a singer, notice your personal developments and inner transformations.

**3** Stay encouraged and inspired by the beautiful and mysterious bond that life and singing share.

*A life best lived is a life lived with JOY.*

A life where music exhilarates our crispest mornings and soothes our coarsest nights. A life not focused myopically on our own gain, but unblinking in our desire to serve others. A life where neither ecstasy nor tragedy monopolize our capacity for hope, but where victories and adversities compete as equals on the heart's battlefield for meaning and purpose.

Such *LIFE* is possible.

Possible when every moan, laugh, sob, cackle, grunt, murmur, chortle, titter, whimper, howl, squeal, gulp, cry, shriek, giggle, prayer, plea, yawp... every single noise... is consecrated to JOY.

**"MAKE A JOYFUL NOISE"** means that your precious voice must no longer remain trapped inside you, but instead must come forth audaciously, daringly, and unapologetically. There are few greater tragedies in life than when a voice goes unheard. Yet, many voices remain captive to fear. Don't let that voice be your voice! Joy is uniquely equipped to cast out these very fears!

Joy is not merely a feeling—it is a *choice* that we make daily against all odds. Joy is the deep *trust* that ultimately, one way or another, everything is going to be okay. Joy is the unrelenting *belief* that although problems, setbacks, and heartbreaks may be great, there will always be something greater.

Nevertheless, choosing, trusting, and believing are far more easily said than done. In reality, our lives are often spent searching for elusive answers. Consider this though—what if life's most important answers aren't found in the searching? What if they are found... in the *being found*?

If you'll allow it, joy can find you in your singing... maybe when you least suspect. It may find you laughing and frolicking. It may find you kicking and screaming. It may find you weeping and mourning. But, no matter how it finds you, joy will overtake your life if you are brave enough to just keep on singing.

**To make a joyful noise**, we must refuse to allow the miraculous to remain imprisoned within us. Only a Creator of endless joy could divide infinity into the digestible morsels of time that we call "the present." And only a Creator of endless song could divide the artistry of the universe into the digestible morsels of heavenly music that we call our voices.

So, I suppose that's why it's up to you.

To see all of that beauty.

To choose not to be silent about it.

To

 Invite joy to become a more powerful force in your singing life than doubt, judgment, or fear.

 Seize any opportunity to make a joyful noise by letting your God-given instrument be *heard*!

 If we've come this far together, then there's nothing left to do other than to **SING LIKE NEVER BEFORE!**

# INDEX

## A

| | |
|---|---|
| abdominal (belly) breathing | **3**, 4-8, 10, 33-34, 37 |
| acid reflux | **73**, 74 |
| actions (objectives) | **83**, 86, 89 |
| acting | 81-85, 87-90 |
| Adam's apple | 11-**12**, 69 |
| ageism | 92 |
| airflow | 1, 3, 6, 8, **9**, 13, 15, 17, 19, 21-22, 25, 27, 28, 30, 41-43, 48, 52, 61-63, 66, 68, 78 |
| alcohol | 73, **74** |
| appoggio breathing | **5**, 6-7, 10, 33-34, 37 |
| approximant consonants | 42, 47, 57, 78 |
| aryepiglottic folds | **20**, 30, 69 |
| aryepiglottic muscle | 20 |
| arytenoid cartilages | **12**, 13, 15-20, 30, 52-57, 61-63, 67-69 |
| arytenoid distortion | 19, **68**, 69 |
| atlas (C1 vertebra) | 40 |
| audience connection | 42, 81-90, 97 |
| authenticity | 42, 64, 81-85, 87-88, 90, 94, 96, 99 |

## B

| | |
|---|---|
| baseline laryngoscopy | 72 |
| belting | 15, 48, 51, 53, 55, **59**, 61, 65 |
| breathing | 1-13, 15-17, 21-22, 24, 31-39, 42-44, 48, 50-53, 57-59, 61-63, 65-66, 68-70, 74-75, 78-80, 86, 89, 90 |
| breath support | 1, 5, **6**, 7-10, 21-22, 33, 36-37, 42-43, 50, 52, 57, 59, 62-63, 65, 68-69, 78 |
| breathiness (aspirate) | 17-18, 52, 54-57, 59, 61, **62**, 63, 67 |
| bright resonances | 20, 25-27, 29, 30, 42-43, 49-50, 56, 59, 64-66, 79 |
| butterfly pose | 33 |

## C

| | |
|---|---|
| cardiovascular exercise | 75 |
| cat/cow pose | 34 |
| character voices | 20, 23, 25-26, 30, 42-43, 57, 66, 69, 79, 85 |
| chest dominant mix | **55**, 59, 61 |
| chest voice (M1) | 15, 48, 51-52, 53, 54-59, 61, 68, 78 |
| chiaroscuro | 20, 25-26, 30, 42, 50, 64, **66** |
| child's pose | 34 |
| chin | 11, 38, **45**, 46 |
| classical singing | 26, 56, 60, 64, 66, 70 |
| clavicular (chest) breathing | **2**, 3, 6, 34-36, 38 |
| clavicle (collarbone) | **2**, 37-39 |
| closed quotient | **51**, 53-54, 59, 61-63 |
| compression | 8-9, 13-15, 17-19, 43, 51-59, **61-63**, 65-69, 75, 80 |
| conductive resonance | **53**, 54, 88 |
| constrictor muscles | 27 |
| contemporary singing | 17, 19, 26, 30, 52, 55-56, 59-70 |
| confidence | 31, 33, 36-37, 60, 78, 87-89, 91-93, 95-97, 99-100 |
| cracking | 54, 56-57, 61 |
| creativity | 82-85, 90, 96 |
| cricoid cartilage | 11, **12**, 13, 16-20, 30, 38, 52-57, 61-69 |
| cricothyroid | 12, **16**, 22, 28, 54-57, 59, 61, 66, 70, 75 |
| cricothyroid joint | **16**, 66 |
| criticism | 95-97 |
| cysts | 67, 72 |

## D

| | |
|---|---|
| dance | 4, 31-33, 75 |
| dark resonances | 20, 25-26, 30, 42-43, 49-50, 60, 64, 66, 79 |
| decompression | 13, 17-18, 43, 51-52, 54-59, 61, **62**, 63, 65-69, 79-80 |
| diaphragm | **1**, 3-5, 10, 17, 75, 86 |
| diction (consonants) | 17-18, 25, 27, 29, 41-44, 47, 57, 61-63, 78, 80 |
| diet ("singer's diet") | 71, **73**, 74 |
| digastric | 38-39, 44-45, **46** |
| distortion (rasp) | 17, 19, 52, 62-63, **67-69** |

## E

| | |
|---|---|
| ears | 21-22, 25, 38, 72 |
| edema | 67 |
| embouchure | 16, 21, 23-25, 27, 41-42, 44-46, **48-50**, 51, 54-56, 58-59 |
| emotion | 23, 52, 67, 81, 83-86, 93, 95, 98-100 |
| emoting | 83-84 |
| ENT doctors | 67, **72**, 73 |
| epiglottic distortion | 69 |
| epiglottis | 13-14, **20**, 26-27, 29, 30, 45, 69, 74 |
| epithelium | **14**, 19, 67 |
| esophagus | 20, 27, 29, 71, 73-74 |
| exhalation | 1-2, 5-10, 13, 17, 21, 24, 33, 36-37, 41-43, 52, 58, 61-63, 78, 86 |
| external intercostals | **4**, 5, 7, 10, 33, 37 |
| extrinsic larynx muscles (def.) | 38 |
| eyes | 88 |

## F

| | |
|---|---|
| false vocal folds | **19**, 68 |
| false vocal fold distortion | 19, **68** |
| falsetto | 51-52, 54-55, 56, 57, 59, 61 |
| fear | 2, 39, 57, 65, 72-73, 78-80, 88-89, 91-92, 96-97, 99-100 |
| feet | **31**, 34, 79 |
| female falsetto | 56 |
| female head voice | **54**, 56-57 |
| flageolet (M3) | 51, **57**, 58, 61 |
| forgiveness | 95 |
| formants | **25**, 27, 30, 48-50, 65-66 |
| frequency | 9, **22**, 25, 54, 57-58 |
| fricative consonants | 7, 8, 10, 25, 41, 63, 75, 78 |

## G

| | |
|---|---|
| genioglossus | 41-43, 46, 49 |
| geniohyoid | 39, 44-45, **46** |
| glottals | **18**, 61 |
| glottic consonants | **17**, 18, 52, 61-62, 78 |
| glottis | **9**, 13-14, 17-18, 20, 61-63 |
| glutes | 16, 33 |
| gratitude | 23, 71, 94, **97** |
| growls | 69 |

## H

| | |
|---|---|
| hard palate | 7, 25, 41 |
| head | 16, 23-24, 37-39, **40**, 41, 45, 54, 60 |
| head dominant mix | 55 |
| head voice (M2) | 16, 48, 51-53, **54**, 55-59, 61-62 |
| hemorrhages | 67, 72 |
| high heels | 34 |
| high larynx positions | 11-12, 16, 26, 29, 30, 39-40, 43-46, 48, 56, 59, 63-64, **65**, 66 |
| high notes | 7, 9, **16**, 22, 28-29, 32, 40, 43-45, 47-48, 50, 53-60, 64, 66, 91, 99 |
| hip movement | 33 |
| hips | 31-32, **33**, 34 |
| hissing | **7**, 8, 10, 25, 41, 63, 75 |
| hydration | **71**, 73-74 |
| hyoglossus | 41-42, **43**, 46, 49, 69 |

| | | | | | | | |
|---|---|---|---|---|---|---|---|
| hyoid bone | 11, **12**, 14, 16, 19-20, 26, 29-30, 32, 38, 39, 41-43, 45-46, 49, 64-66, 68-69 | laryngoscopy | 72 | monotone speech | **80**, 85 | pelvis | 3, 5, 10, 31-32, **33**, 34-35 |
| | | larynx positions | 2-3, **11**, 12-13, 15-21, 23-24, 26-27, 29-30, 37-40, 42-48, 51, 56-66, 68-70, 72-75, 79 | mouth | 7, 16, 21, 23-26, **27**, 28, 41, 43-46, 48-50, 58, 60, 64, 71-72 | perfectionism | 67, 87, 89-90, 91, 94-95, **96**, 97-98 |
| **I** | | | | mucosal wave | **13**, 14, 51, 57-58 | performance anxiety (nerves) | 2, 22, 32, 44, 86, 88, **89**, 91, 97, 99 |
| identifying the scene partner | **82**, 83 | larynx | 11-12, 16, 21, 23, 26-27, 29-30, 39-40, 42-46, 48, 51, 56, 59, 61-63, **64-66**, 79 | mucous membrane | **13**, 14, 19 | pharynx | 21, 23-25, **26-28**, 29-30, 41-42, 44-45, 49, 60, 64-66, 72 |
| imagination | 82-84 | | | mucus | 71 | | |
| inhalation | 1-9, 17, 21, 35-38, 42, 58, 78, 86 | larynx tension | 2-3, 8-9, 16, 29-30, 37-40, 42-44, 46-48, 62-66, 68-69, 75 | mylohyoid | 38-39, 44-45, **46** | physical fitness | 4, 71, 73, **75**, 77, 79, 93 |
| inhale phonation | 1, **58** | | | **N** | | pigeon pose | 33 |
| intrinsic larynx muscles (*def.*) | 38 | lateral cricoarytenoid | 12-13, **18**, 52, 55-56, 61, 63 | nasal cavity | 21, 23-24, 26, **28**, 29-30, 41, 53, 60, 72, 88 | pitch | 9, 15-16, **22**, 23, 28, 40-41, 43-44, 48, 50, 52-54, 56-60, 64-66, 68, 70, 80 |
| interarytenoids | 12-13, 18, 52, 55-56, 61, 63 | lateral pterygoid | 45 | nasal consonants | 19, 25, 29, **41**, 47, 57, 68, 78 | playing the action | **83**, 84, 89 |
| intercostal (rib) breathing | **4**, 5-7, 10, 33-35, 37 | lips | 7, 21, 23-25, 41, 48, **50**, 55, 58, 63, 86 | nasal resonance | 19, 21, 24, 28-29, **30**, 41, 50, 55, 57, 59, 65, 68, 88 | playing the emotion | **83**, 84 |
| internal intercostals | 4-5, 7, **10**, 33, 37 | lip embouchure (position) | 16, 21, 23-25, 45, 48, **50**, 55-56, 58, 63 | nasality | 20, 28-29, **30**, 66 | playing the opposite | 84 |
| **J** | | listening | 21-25, 42, 51, 53, 73, 79, 91, 93 | nasopharynx | 26-27, **28**, 29-30, 41 | plié | 32 |
| | | loud environments | 74, 79, **80** | neck | 2-3, 5, 11, 16, 30, 37-38, **39**, 40, 44-45, 53, 60, 75, 79 | plosive consonants | 25, 47, **61**, 78 |
| jaw | 16, 21, 23, 25, 27, 38-41, 44-48, 55, 58, 61, 63, 79 | low larynx positions | 11-12, 26, 29-30, 39, 42-43, 61-63, **66**, 79 | neck tension | 2-3, 16, 30, 37-40, 44-45, 63, 75, 79 | polyps | 67, 72 |
| jaw/tongue separation | 47 | low notes | 9, 15, 16, 22, 28, 40, 52-53, 60, 64 | neutral larynx positions | 12, **64**, 65-66 | posterior cricoarytenoids | 12-13, **17**, 18, 55, 62-63 |
| jaw bulging | 43, **46** | lower back | 5, 32-33, **34**, 40 | neutral jaw position | 41, **44**, 46, 48 | posture (alignment) | 2, 5-6, 31-40, 44-45, 61, 75, 79 |
| jaw embouchure (position) | 21, 23, 25, 27, 41, 44-46, **48**, 50, 55, 61 | lower back breathing | 5, **34** | NG consonant | 29, **41**, 43, 47, 57, 78 | practice | 16, 18, 22-23, 33, 39, 41, 44, 47-48, 56, 58, 60-61, 63, 66, 70-71, 73, **76**, 77, 79, 86, 90-91, 93-94, 98-99 |
| jaw tension | 16, 38-41, 44-48, 63, 79 | lungs | 1-2, 4-5, 7, 9, 11-13, 17, 20-21, 23, 26, 28, 48, 74-75, 78 | NG tongue position | **41**, 43 | | |
| jaw thrusting | 16, **45**, 79 | | | nodules (nodes) | 67, 72 | preparation | 77, 85-86, 89, **90** |
| joy | 2, 92, 98-99, **100** | lung volume (*def.*) | 9 | nose | **28**, 29-30, 72, 88 | puckering | **50**, 58 |
| judgment | 57, 60, 73, 78-79, 87, 89-90, 93-94, 96-97 | **M** | | **O** | | **Q** | |
| **K** | | male head voice | **54**, 56 | obliques | 3, 33 | quadratus lumborum | 33-34 |
| knee pedaling | 32 | "making it" | 93-94, **98** | omohyoid | 39 | | |
| knees | 31, **32**, 34 | mandible (*def.*) | 45 | onsets | 17-18, 52, 58, 61-62, 70, 78 | **R** | |
| knurdle (knödel) | 43 | marking | 77 | oropharynx | 26, **27**, 28, 42 | *raccogliere la bocca* | 44 |
| **L** | | masque | 16, 53-54, 88 | open quotient | **51**, 54, 56-57, 59, 61-63 | raked stages | 34 |
| | | masseter | 44 | | | range | 7, 9, 15-16, 22, 28-29, 40-41, 43-44, 47-48, 50-57, 59, **60**, 64-66, 68, 70, 74, 78, 80 |
| lamina propria | **14**, 19, 22, 67, 71 | mastoid process | **38**, 46 | **P** | | | |
| laryngeal tilt | 16 | medial pterygoid | 45 | palatoglossus | **41**, 42-43, 46, 49 | rectus abdominis | 3, 8, **10**, 33, 37 |
| laryngopharynx | **26**, 27-28, 64-66 | microphone | 26, 60, 65-66, 68-69 | passion | 91-93, 95, 98-100 | registration | 15, 20, 29, 44, 48, 50, **51**, 52-62, 68, 70, 74, 78-80 |
| | | mix voice | 51-54, **55**, 56, 59, 61 | patella | 11 | | |

| | | | | | | | |
|---|---|---|---|---|---|---|---|
| reinforced falsetto | 54, **56**, 59, 61 | strain | 2-3, 6, 8-9, 16-18, 37-40, 42-48, 50, 52-53, 59, 62-69, 75, 78, 80 | tongue tension | 16, 38-43, 45, 47, 49, 63, 69 | vowels | 18, **25**, 27, 29, 41, 44, 47-50, 52, 57, 61-62, 68, 78 |
| relaxation/reducing tension | 2-3, 6, 8-10, 16-17, 27, 30, 32-48, 52, 59, 62-64, 66-68, 75, 77-80, 86, 88-89 | | | tongue tip | 7, 41, 47, 63 | | |
| | | stretching | 33-35, **39**, 44, 75, 79, 89 | trachea | 1, **12**, 13, 18-20, 38, 63, 74 | **W** | |
| resonance | 9, 15-16, 20-23, **24**, 25-30, 40-45, 48-51, 53-55, 57, 59-62, 65-66, 68, 79, 88 | style | 19, 23, 26, 42, 48, 52, 55-56, 59-60, 62, 64-70, 76, 81, 85, 90-91 | transverse abdominis | **3**, 10, 33 | water | **71**, 73-74 |
| | | styloglossus | 41, **42**, 43, 46, 49 | tremolo | 70 | weight training | 8, 13, **75** |
| ribs | 1, **4**, 5-7, 10, 32-37 | stylohyoid | 39 | trills | 24, 41, 57, 63, 75 | whistle voice | 51, 57, **58** |
| **S** | | styloid process | 42 | true artistry | 81-83, 85-87, 90, 94, 96, 98, 100 | wobble | 70 |
| scapulae | **35**, 36-37 | subglottic pressure | 3, 6-8, **9**, 10, 13, 19, 21, 42-45, 50, 52, 57, 59, 63, 65, 70, 75 | trust | 78, 86-87, 90, 94, 99-100 | **Y** | |
| shoulders | 2-3, 35, **36**, 37-38, 40, 44 | | | twang | 20, 26-27, 29, **30**, 56, 59, 64-65, 68, 79 | yawning | 11-12, 26, 64, **66** |
| singing is a gift | 23, 86, 91-93, 95, **97**, 100 | swallowing | 11-12, 19, **20**, 27, 29, 43, 46, 64, 71, 73-74 | **U** | | yoga | 33-34, 75, 79, 89 |
| singing is a sport | 93 | sympathetic resonance | 24, **53**, 54 | | | | |
| smoking | 74 | | | upper back | **35**, 36-37 | | |
| song monologue work | 85 | **T** | | uvular consonants | 69, 78 | | |
| snarling | 50 | temporal muscle | 44 | **V** | | | |
| snoring | 28 | temporal mandibular disorder (TMD) | 44 | Valsalva maneuver | **8**, 13, 19, 75 | | |
| soft palate (velum) | 21, 23, 27-28, **29**, 30, 41, 44, 49-50, 55, 61, 69 | temporal mandibular joint (TMJ) | 44 | velar distortion | 69 | | |
| solar plexus | 8 | | | vestibular/ventricular folds (*def.*) | 19 | | |
| song lyrics | 47, 81-83, 85-86, 89-90 | throat | 19-20, **26-28**, 30, 42-43, 69, 71-74 | vibrato | 70 | | |
| soul | 81, 86-87, 90, 93, 96, 98, 100 | thyroarytenoid | 12, 14, **15**, 19, 45, 52-56, 59, 61, 63, 68, 70, 75 | vocal damage | 67, 71, **72**, 73-74, 79-80 | | |
| sound waves | 13, 16, **21**, 22, 24, 30, 53, 57, 86 | thyroid cartilage | **11**, 12-20, 26, 29-30, 38-39, 45, 52-54, 56-57, 61-68 | vocal folds | 6, 8-9, 11-12, **13-14**, 15-24, 28, 30, 39, 42-43, 48, 51-75, 78-80 |
| speech | 11-13, 17-18, 25-27, 42, 47, 49, 52-53, 61, 64, 68-70, 74, **78-80**, 85 | thyrohyoid | 39 | vocal health | 14, 44, 52-54, 59, 62-69, 71-80 | | |
| | | thyromuscularis | 12, 14, **15**, 52-53, 68 | vocal friendship | 78, 89, 92, **94**, 95, 97-98, 100 | | |
| spine | 31-32, 34-37, 40 | thyrovocalis (vocalis) | 12, 14, 15, 52-56, 61, 63, 68 | vocal fry | 51, **52**, 57-58, 61, 68, 80 | | |
| spontaneity | 33, 80, **90** | timbre | **23**, 60 | vocal fry distortion | 52, 62-63, **68** | | |
| spreading | 16, 45, **50**, 55-56 | tongue (glossus) | 7, 16, 21, 23, 25, 27-29, 38-43, 45, 47-49, 58, 63, 69 | vocal journey | 87-89, 91, 92, 94-95, 97-98, **99**, 100 | | |
| specificity | 76, 82-83 | | | vocal rest | **77**, 79 | | |
| staccato | 70 | tongue base (root) | 27, 29, 41-43, 47, 49, 63, 69 | vocal scars | 78, **95**, 97-99 | | |
| stage presence | 2, 4, 31-33, 36-37, 78, 81-90 | tongue embouchure (position) | 21, 23, 25, **27**, 41-43, 48-50, 63 | voice types (Fachs) | 60 | | |
| sternocleidomastoid | **38**, 39 | | | *voix mixte* | 51, 55 | | |
| sternohyoid | 39, 66 | tongue retraction | 29, 42, 43, 49, 63, 69 | volume (dynamics) | 3, 6, 9, 15-18, 21, 24-26, 42, 44-45, 48, 50, 52-53, 55-57, 59, 60-66, 68-69, 74, 77-80 |
| sternothyroid | 39 | tongue squeezing | 16, **43**, 69 | | | | |
| sternum | 1, 4-6, 8, **37** | tongue stretching | 39, 43 | | | | |
| straight tone | 70 | | | | | | |

# ACKNOWLEDGMENTS

### JUSTIN STONEY

Special thanks to:

My inspirations: Dr. Scott McCoy, Dr. Johan Sundberg, and Dr. Ingo Titze
My teachers: Richard Fracker, Aaron Hagan, David Jones, and Ralph Williams
My colleagues: Zac Bradford, Brendan Houdek, Matthew Johnson, and John West
My family: Elenka Raschkow, Carolyn Stoney, and Manny Stoney

This book would not have been possible without your expertise, guidance, time, and love.

### MARK PATE

Throughout the creation of this book I have had two constant sources of support, without which I could not have done this. First (chronologically at least) are my parents, John and Peggy. Never once did you try to dissuade me in my pursuit of a career in illustration. For that I am eternally shocked and grateful.

Second is my best friend, Elizabeth who, between the beginning and end of this project, became my wife. Your selfless love, encouragement, and support amazes me everyday.

# ABOUT THE AUTHOR

NewYorkVocalCoaching.com // VoiceTeacherTraining.com // VoiceLessonsToTheWorld.com // JustinStoney.com

Justin Stoney is the founder of New York Vocal Coaching and the developer of the NYVC Voice Teacher Training & Certification Program.

He has taught thousands of singers and voice teachers of diverse backgrounds, levels, styles, ethnicities, nationalities, and ages. His clients also include Emmy, Grammy, Oscar, and Tony Award-winning artists.

Mr. Stoney has been invited as a keynote speaker and presenter for national and international conferences and workshops, including PAVA (Pan American Vocology Association), ViP (Vocology in Practice), and the NYSTA (New York Singing Teachers' Association) Professional Development Program. He has appeared on numerous media outlets, including NBC, CBS, and ABC, and been featured in multiple publications, including *The New York Times*, *Esquire*, and *SELF*. He is a member of NATS (National Association of Teachers of Singing), ViP, PAVA, VASTA (Voice and Speech Trainers Association), The Voice Foundation, Actors' Equity, and SAG-AFTRA. Justin also collaborates with leading voice doctors and laryngologists to help bridge the gap between vocal pedagogy and voice medicine, and participates in new research studies on vocal science, pedagogy, and technology.

Justin is also the creator and host of the popular singing shows *Voice Lessons to the World* and *Quick Singing Tips*. These shows offer vocal information and training to singers from across the globe who may not otherwise have access to professional singing instruction.

He is grateful for the God-given opportunity to help vocalists from all over the world to "Make a Joyful Noise!"

# ABOUT THE ILLUSTRATOR

dude_huge     The_Hugest_Dude     dude-huge

Mark Pate is an award-winning illustrator living and working in Queens, New York with his best friend and wife, Elizabeth. He grew up in Mesa, Arizona with a passion for sequential story-telling and received a BFA with a focus in drawing from Arizona State University. Mark has worked as a freelance illustrator for over 10 years. His past work includes storyboard art for film and television, character/environment concept art, illustration for animation, and sequential art for comic books.

In addition to his illustration work, Mark is the Associate Director of the Transform artist residency organization which hosts art residencies across the country. In his work, Mark hopes to elicit joy, laughter, and thoughtful reflection while representing the under-represented and lifting up the voice of the voiceless.

## 10,000 Reasons (Bless The Lord)
### Song by Matt Redman

The sun comes up
It's a new day dawning
It's time to sing Your song again
Whatever may pass
And whatever lies before me
Let me be singing
When the evening comes

Bless the Lord O my soul
O my soul
Worship His Holy name
**SING LIKE NEVER BEFORE**
O my soul
I'll worship Your Holy name

You're rich in love
And You're slow to anger
Your name is great
And Your heart is kind
For all Your goodness
I will keep on singing
Ten thousand reasons
For my heart to find

Bless the Lord O my soul
O my soul
Worship His Holy name
**SING LIKE NEVER BEFORE**
O my soul
I'll worship Your Holy name

And on that day
When my strength is failing
The end draws near
And my time has come
Still my soul will
Sing Your praise unending
Ten thousand years
And then forevermore

Bless the Lord O my soul
O my soul
Worship His Holy name
**SING LIKE NEVER BEFORE**
O my soul
I'll worship Your Holy name